Strategy in 3D

Strategy in 3D

Essential Tools to Diagnose, Decide, and Deliver

Greg Fisher, John E. Wisneski, and Rene M. Bakker

OXFORD
UNIVERSITY PRESS

OXFORD
UNIVERSITY PRESS

Oxford University Press is a department of the University of Oxford. It furthers the University's objective of excellence in research, scholarship, and education by publishing worldwide. Oxford is a registered trade mark of Oxford University Press in the UK and certain other countries.

Published in the United States of America by Oxford University Press
198 Madison Avenue, New York, NY 10016, United States of America.

© Oxford University Press 2020

Library of Congress Cataloging-in-Publication Data
Names: Fisher, Greg (Gregory Campbell), 1976– author. |
Wisneski, John E., author. | Bakker, Rene M., 1982– author.
Title: Strategy in 3D : essential tools to diagnose, decide, and deliver /
by Greg Fisher, John E. Wisneski, Rene M. Bakker.
Description: New York, NY : Oxford University Press, [2019] |
Includes bibliographical references and index.
Identifiers: LCCN 2019053117 (print) | LCCN 2019053118 (ebook) |
ISBN 9780190081478 (hardback) | ISBN 9780190081485 (paperback) |
ISBN 9780190081508 (epub) | ISBN 9780197521847
Subjects: LCSH: Strategic planning.
Classification: LCC HD30.28 .F5723 2019 (print) | LCC HD30.28 (ebook) |
DDC 658.4/012—dc23
LC record available at https://lccn.loc.gov/2019053117
LC ebook record available at https://lccn.loc.gov/2019053118

1 3 5 7 9 8 6 4 2

To our family and friends for their unfaltering love and support, and the many colleagues any former students whose constant feedback guided our thinking.

Contents

Figures

Tables

1
Introduction

It used to be that strategy was the domain of only those at the very top of an organization. It used to be that strategy happened at off-site retreats (often coupled with golf, cigars, and scotch; Figure 1.1). It used to be that strategy was only discussed as part of an annual planning cycle. It used to be that strategy was about grand, long-term plans that stretched way into the future. It used to be that strategy was largely cerebral.

Figure 1.1. The good ol' days of strategic management.

Forget the way it used to be.

The current business environment does not wait for companies to slowly adjust. The relentless pace of change renders today's long-term future tomorrow's history. Rapid innovations and ever-increasing complexities limit executives' ability to know everything about everyone. And this leads to problems for the "old" model of strategy. Does this mean strategy is no longer useful, or even feasible?

No.

Good strategists are needed now *more than ever.* But what today's high-performing organizations do is very different from what they used to do. These companies (1) make strategy *part of every manager's role*; (2) strategize *continuously*—planned, unplanned, and on the go; and (3) tackle strategic problems through individuals from *all parts of the organization.*

Strategy in this new, fast-paced world is about *diagnosing* the diverse array of complex challenges confronting organizations, *deciding* on novel solutions to address those challenges, and *delivering* by taking action on those solutions. This forms the very pillar of the 3D approach to strategy that is central to this book.

What We Offer

This book presents the most critical tools and frameworks that are well developed and time tested and builds on them by offering relevant, applicable, and understandable applications through recent extensions and cases.

Tying into our belief that specific situations require specific, and usually quick, strategic actions, the approach we take is heavily tools based. Some of these tools are extremely well known (think STEEP, SWOT, and five forces, for example); others are maybe less so. Regardless of their prevalence, all the tools we draw on were designed to assist strategists in dealing with ambiguous or complex business challenges or tapping anticipated opportunities. Each tool is one that can be added to the repertoire or "toolbox" of a strategist as he or she sees fit. Some of the tools are narrow in scope, others broad. We organize the tools by the 3Ds that make up the 3D framework—diagnose, decide, deliver. That is, when confronted with a specific diagnosis question—for example, "What is the most relevant current threat in our environment?"—this book will highlight what tools and frameworks are at your disposal. And when we say "answer," we do not mean just coming up with an off-the-cuff best guess in a brief email to management. What we mean is coming up with a rigorous response that is rooted in thorough analysis and presented using relevant data, visuals, and persuasive logic.

The key is this: the field of strategy in the current day and age has become more relevant (not less), it should be practiced by more people (not fewer), and its functional domain should be broadened (not narrowed). Anyone with career ambition in the business world needs to become a strategist. We hope this book will serve as a useful resource for everyone willing to take that leap.

Part I of the book provides insight into fundamental strategy concepts and ideas. In this part of the book we define strategy in a business context and discuss how strategy is enacted in different ways at different levels of an organization Thereafter we describe each of the three elements that are central to being strategic within a business—the 3Ds of diagnose, decide, and deliver—and we discuss the subcomponents underlying each of these elements.

Part II of the book outlines a series of tools that could and should form part of a manager's strategy toolbox. It outlines tools that enable managers to overcome biases and be systematic, analytical, and creative in solving strategic challenges and seizing strategic opportunities.

PART I
FUNDAMENTALS

2
Definition and Levels of Strategy

Definition of Strategy

What exactly is strategy? Strategy is a term that has been used in business since the 1960s, yet it was only really formalized as a business school discipline after the publication of Michael Porter's books, *Competitive Strategy* in 1980 and *Competitive Advantage* in 1985. It is a term borrowed from the military, where the concept of strategy has been used in planning for war for more than 2000 years. Over the past 50 years, the concept of strategy has become a central and overarching concept in business, influencing some of the most important and impactful business decisions during that time. The following are a number of different definitions of strategy from influential scholars and practitioners over the years.

Definition 1 by Kenneth Andrews in 1971: "Strategy is the pattern of decisions in a company that determines and reveals its objectives, purposes, or goals, produces the principal policies and plan for achieving those goals, and defines the range of business the company is to pursue, the kind of economic and human organization it is or intends to be, and the nature of the economic and noneconomic contribution it intends to make to its shareholders, employees, customers, and communities."[1]

Definition 2 by Michael Porter in 1980: "[Strategy is] a broad formula for how a business is going to compete, what its goals should be, and what policies will be needed to carry out those goals. Strategy is about the creation and capture of value."[2]

Definition 3 by Richard Rumelt in 2011: "Strategy contains three elements:

1. A diagnosis that defines or explains the nature of the challenge. A good diagnosis simplifies the often-overwhelming complexity of reality by identifying certain aspects of the situation as critical.
2. A guiding policy for dealing with the challenge. This is an overall approach chosen to cope with or overcome the obstacles identified in the diagnosis.
3. A set of coherent actions that are designed to carry out the guiding policy. These are steps that are coordinated with one another to work together in accomplishing the guiding policy."[3]

Definition 4 by A. G. Lafley and Roger Martin in 2013: "[Strategy is] an integrated set of choices which position a business in its industry so as to create sustainable advantage and superior returns."[4]

From across these definitions, we determine that strategy consists of three primary elements:

1. Identifying and describing a challenge or opportunity confronting a business—the *diagnosis* element
2. Making a decision about what will be done to deal with and overcome the central challenge or capture the key opportunity—the *decide* element
3. Devising and implementing a coherent set of actions to deliver on key decisions—the *deliver* element

Integrating these three elements into a single definition, we define strategy in a business context as follows:

Strategy is a *diagnosis* that defines or explains a business challenge or opportunity, a *decision* or set of *decisions* for dealing with the challenge or opportunity, and a coherent set of actions to *deliver* on the decisions so as to create sustainable advantage and superior returns.

Levels of Strategy

The concept of strategy plays out and is relevant at different levels of an organization—the corporate, business, and managerial levels. It has a different orientation and focus at each of these different levels. The differences between the three levels of strategy are described next and summarized in Table 2.1.

Corporate-Level Strategy

Corporate-level strategy is concerned with the selection of business areas in which the company should compete and with the development and coordination of that portfolio of businesses. It is relevant in diversified firms, which operate multiple different businesses

Table 2.1 Summary Comparison of Different Levels of Strategy

	Corporate-Level Strategy	Business-Level Strategy	Managerial-Level Strategic Decision-Making
Who	C-level executives	Business/division presidents	All managers and potentially other employees
When	Cyclical—annual or quarterly	Cyclical—annual or quarterly	Continuous
How	Top-down from mission and values	Top-down following *MOST*: *Mission Objectives Strategies Tactics*	Bottom-up using insights developed from strategic analyses
What	Strategic plan	Annual operating plan (AOP)	Value proposition expressed as tangible and intangible benefits in excess of invested costs

across various industries. Corporate-level strategy is generally the focus of high-level corporate executives.

Business-Level Strategy

Business-level strategy is about developing and sustaining a competitive advantage in delivering an identifiable set of products and/or services. It is relevant for a single business in a larger corporation or for a firm with a single business providing related offerings. Business-level strategy is the focus of business owners, entrepreneurs, and business unit leaders in a larger corporation.

Managerial-Level Strategic Decision-Making

Managerial-level strategic decision-making is concerned with identifying and dealing with a diverse range of strategic challenges and opportunities confronting a business. It involves tackling challenges or opportunities that may have an impact on business performance. It is the focus of managers at various levels of an organization. Managerial-level strategic decision-making requires two core skills: analytical thinking (using a structured yet creative approach to working through issues) and communicating recommendations (being clear, concise, and compelling).

Almost all of the tools and concepts that are introduced and discussed in this textbook can be applied to address managerial-, business-, and corporate-level strategic issues. Many of these tools were initially developed to tackle business- and corporate-level strategy issues but have been adapted to facilitate managerial-level strategic decision-making.

3

The Context for Strategic Decision-Making

Strategic decisions, whether they are at the managerial, business, or corporate level, are not made in a vacuum. They are strongly influenced by and often dependent on certain organizational and environmental attributes. Hence, any person making a strategic decision needs to be acutely aware of organizational and environmental factors that may significantly impact how things are perceived within an organization. These factors may include the organizational mission, vision, and values. They may also include the resources, capabilities, core competencies, and activities embedded within an organization. This chapter defines each of these factors and presents the concept of competitive advantage.

Vision, Mission, and Values

A strategy is forged in the context of a firm's vision, mission, and values.

Vision defines a desired future state of a firm, articulating in bold terms what the company would like to achieve. Microsoft's vision, in its early days, was *a computer on every desk and in every home.*[1] Teach for America's vision is *one day, all children in this nation will have the opportunity to attain an excellent education.*[2]

A *mission* describes what a company does or strives to do; it is a statement of purpose. Google's mission is *to organize the world's information and make it universally accessible and useful.*[3] McKinsey and Company describe their mission as follows: *Our mission is to help our clients make distinctive, lasting, and substantial improvements in their performance and to build a great firm that attracts, develops, excites, and retains exceptional people.*[4]

Values state how people within a firm should conduct themselves, how they should do business, and what kinds of things they should care about and pay attention to. McKinsey and Company describe their values as follows:

- *Adhere to the highest professional standards*
  - put client interests ahead of the firm's
  - observe high ethical standards
  - preserve client confidences
  - maintain an independent perspective
  - manage client and firm resources cost-effectively
- *Improve our clients' performance significantly*
  - follow the top-management approach
  - use our global network to deliver the best of the firm to all clients
  - bring innovations in management practice to clients
  - build client capabilities to sustain improvement
  - build enduring relationships based on trust
- *Create an unrivaled environment for exceptional people*
  - be nonhierarchical and inclusive
  - sustain a caring meritocracy
  - develop one another through apprenticeship and mentoring
  - uphold the obligation to dissent
  - govern ourselves as a "one firm" partnership[5]

Vision, mission, and values are NOT strategy. They do, however, create the context within which strategies are created, evaluated, and implemented. Vision, mission, and values serve as key input into strategy diagnosis, decision-making, and delivery.

Resources, Capabilities, Core Competencies, and Activities

A strategy often leverages, or seeks to build, a firm's resources, capabilities, and core competencies.

Resources are assets (things that a firm has access to) that it can draw on when formulating and implementing a strategy. Resources can be tangible (having physical attributes and being visible) or intangible (not having physical attributes and being invisible). Typical resources that may be found within a business include the items listed in Table 3.1.

Capabilities are organizational managerial skills used to orchestrate a diverse set of resources and deploy them in a way that creates value. Capabilities are by nature intangible. They are things that a firm can do and manifest through its structure, routines, and culture.

Core competencies are unique strengths embedded within a firm; they allow a firm to differentiate its products or services such that the firm can create greater value for customers and/or produce output at a lower cost. Core competencies can be the source of competitive advantage.[6]

Examples of core competencies of some well-known businesses can be found in Table 3.2.

Activities are distinct, identifiable, and specific business processes, the things that a business does repeatedly to create and deliver value to clients. Each distinct activity enables a firm to add incremental

Table 3.1 Examples of Tangible and Intangible Business Resources

Tangible Resources	Intangible Resources
Visible, Physical Attributes	*Invisible, No Physical Attributes*
• Capital • Land • Buildings • Plant • Equipment • Supplies • Labor	• Knowledge • Brand • Culture • Reputation • Intellectual property (patents, copyrights, trademarks, trade secrets)

Table 3.2 Example of Core Competencies

Company	Core Competency
Apple	Leveraging industrial design to integrate hardware and software in innovative and category-defining mobile devices that take the user's experience to a new level
Honda	Designing and manufacturing small, but powerful, and highly reliable internal combustion engines
IKEA	Designing and manufacturing functional home furnishings at low prices offered in a unique retail environment
Starbucks	Providing high-quality beverages and selected food items, combined with superior customer service, in a friendly and welcoming environment
UPS	Providing superior supply chain and logistics management services and solutions at a low cost

Adapted from Rothaermel, F. T. *Strategic Management: Concepts.* (New York, NY: McGraw-Hill Education, 2016).

value by transforming inputs into goods and services. Examples of some typical business activities include making sales, ordering inventory, manufacturing, assembly, delivery, invoicing, etc.

Competitive Advantage

Competitive advantage is a central concept in strategy. To follow are some definitions of competitive advantage from various scholars and practitioners:

> *Definition 1 from Richard Rumelt:* "If your business can produce at a lower cost than competitors, or if it can deliver more value than competitors, or a mix of the two, then you have competitive advantage."[7]
>
> *Definition 2 from Joan Magretta:* "Competitive advantage is not about trouncing rivals; it's about creating superior value. The term is both concrete and specific. If you have a real competitive advantage it means that compared with rivals, you operate at a lower cost, command a premium price, or both."[8]

Definition 3 from Jay Barney and William Hesterley: "A firm
has competitive advantage when it is able to create more economic value than rival firms. Economic value is the difference between the perceived benefits gained by a customer that
purchases a firm's products or services and the full economic
cost of producing these products or services."[9]

Definition 4 from Charles Hill, Gareth Jones, and Melissa Schilling:
"A firm is said to have a competitive advantage over its rivals
when its profitability is greater than the average profitability
and profit growth of other companies competing for the same
set of customers. The higher its profitability relative to rivals,
the greater its competitive advantage."[10]

Competitive advantage may be depicted as stemming from differentiation, which allows a firm to charge more for its products or services but
often costs more to produce. The key is to generate better margins from
the differentiated product. Competitive advantage may also stem from
producing a product or service at a lower cost and therefore charging
customers a lower price than alternatives. It may also stem from jointly
reducing cost and increasing customers' willingness to pay, thereby
charging higher prices. This is a dual advantage strategy. These three
strategies—differentiation, low cost, and dual advantage—are depicted
relative to an industry average competitor in Figure 3.1.

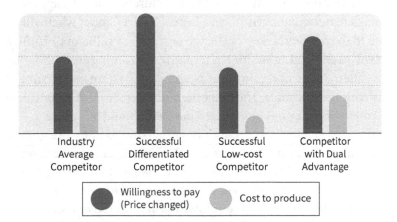

| Industry Average Competitor | Successful Differentiated Competitor | Successful Low-cost Competitor | Competitor with Dual Advantage |

● Willingness to pay (Price changed)   ○ Cost to produce

Figure 3.1. Three types of competitive advantage.

4

The 3Ds of Strategy

As described previously, the definition of strategy is a *diagnosis* that defines or explains a business challenge or opportunity, a *decision* or set of *decisions* for dealing with the challenge or opportunity, and a coherent set of actions to *deliver* on the decisions so as to create sustainable advantage and superior returns. At the core of this definition are three central elements: diagnose, decide, and deliver. These are the three elements that are central to the strategic management process—what we refer to as the 3Ds.

The *diagnose* element entails using an analytical approach to understand a business challenge or to assess the nature of an opportunity confronting a business. It typically involves assessing and connecting external and internal factors impacting a business and using them as a basis to understand the root cause underlying a challenge or opportunity. The outcome of the diagnosing element is a statement or question that distills the core issue confronting a business.

The *decide* element entails using a structured, analytical approach to make reasoned, insightful, and logical choices about what will be done to overcome the key challenge or to seize on the opportunity. It involves generating solution alternatives, screening and validating those alternatives, and using that as a basis to make an impactful and well-considered choice. The outcome of the decide element is a clear statement of policy or choice that a business should pursue.

The *deliver* element entails designing solutions to integrate a policy or choice into a business and then taking coherent action to implement that solution. It may also necessitate that managers defend their solution to others in the business to garner resources and require that the impact of the solution be monitored and evaluated, such that adjustments can be made where necessary. The outcome of the deliver phase is the implementation of a new strategic initiative within a business.

Next, we describe each of the 3D elements and their sub-components in much greater detail.

Diagnose

The first D, diagnose, entails using an analytical approach to truly understand the root cause of a business challenge or the true nature of an opportunity confronting a firm. It is a critical starting point when addressing a strategic issue, yet it is also an element of strategy that can often be overlooked, skirted around, or done only superficially if one is rushed, lazy, or unfocused in the strategy process. Effective strategic diagnoses will ensure that one is working on the right issues to address the challenges or opportunities that are relevant and meaningful. Many times, people within an organization will initially only recognize the surface-level symptoms of a challenge or opportunity, but without a deeper dive to analytically assess the root causes underlying the issue at hand, the true nature of that challenge or opportunity may never be uncovered. This means that many strategies and strategic responses may end up addressing the wrong issue and hence never solve a real problem or leverage a true opportunity.

Diagnoses typically involve assessing and connecting external issues (factors in the environment surrounding a business such as macro trends, market conditions, technology changes, and industry dynamics) with internal issues (factors inside a business such as competencies, resources, internal processes, and firm-specific weaknesses) impacting business outcomes and using them as a basis to understand the root cause underlying a challenge or opportunity. The outcome of the diagnosing element is a statement or question that distills the core issue confronting a business. This question feeds directly into the follow-on process of *deciding* what to do in response to the identified challenge or opportunity.

Key Concepts

Although the issues and opportunities confronting an organization vary wildly, the processes by which one can assess and diagnose them are somewhat structured. The concepts discussed in this section are core in the process of *diagnosing* business challenges or opportunities. While these concepts may be perceived as somewhat progressive from one to the next, seldom does a diagnosis process progress in such a linear way. The process is much more iterative, meaning that discoveries in one element may prompt revisiting other diagnosis elements. These concepts reflect the key ideas that form part of that iterative process.

Recognize potential challenges and opportunities. To begin assessing a strategic issue, one first needs to identify a potential challenge or opportunity. A potential challenge or opportunity may come to the attention of a manager through a variety of different channels including top-down, bottom-up, outside-in, or inside-out. Via the *top-down channel*, a senior executive (or other high-up person in an organization) may make a manager aware of an impending challenge or opportunity and ask the manager to address it. The *bottom-up channel* may come into effect when a front-line employee brings a critical challenge or opportunity to a manager, something the employee has observed in his or her day-to-day tasks and interactions. *The outside-in channel* entails a manager learning about a strategic challenge or opportunity from a customer or someone else outside of the organization. The *inside-out channel* entails a manager recognizing a key strategic challenge or opportunity confronting the organization in his or her role within the firm. The main point here is that managers may be made aware of challenges or opportunities in a multitude of different ways, and it is incumbent on them to act on those initial insights to truly understand the nature of the challenge or opportunity before making definitive decisions about what to do. The outcome of the recognition element is an initial statement about the organizational or environmental symptoms that suggest that there may be a strategic challenge or opportunity for a firm.

Analyze the external environment. With an initial idea about a potential strategic challenge or opportunity for a firm, it is important to understand how the environment beyond the boundaries of a firm may be impacting the focal issue. This entails analyzing what's going on at various different layers beyond an organization's boundary. At the broadest level, it is important to systematically assess trends in the general environment, which may include assessing the impact of economic, technological, social, and political trends on the organization. Narrowing in from the general environment, one should also assess the broader industry in which a firm operates. This may include assessing key relationships between industry participants, including those higher up and further down in the value chain (i.e., suppliers and buyers). Narrowing in even further, it is useful to assess the competitive landscape affecting a firm, which includes understanding the ambitions, intentions, strengths, and weaknesses of the key competitors to the focal firm.

Analyze the internal context. In addition to assessing and understanding the external environment in which a firm operates, it is also important to assess and understand issues *within* a firm. This includes a critical analysis of the firm's resources and capabilities and the structural and procedural issues within the organization that may create barriers or opportunities for success. Internal analysis entails asking the question: "What's going on inside an organization that may be impacting firm competitiveness or may be a source of competitiveness in the future?" Managers can utilize a variety of tools and frameworks to systematically assess the known and hidden strengths and weaknesses in an organization and link these with key external factors as a basis to identify root causes and key insights.

Identify root causes and key insights. The key outcome of the diagnosis phase is an identification and clear description of the root cause and key insights giving rise to challenges and opportunities within a firm. To do this, it is useful to carefully consider and integrate important information from the external and internal analysis to identify the initiating cause of a challenge or opportunity. True root causes are often revealed by asking "why" multiple times. This was a technique developed and fine-tuned within the Toyota Motor Corporation as a critical component of its problem solving. Taiichi Ohno, the architect of the Toyota Production System in the 1950s, described the method in his book *Toyota Production System: Beyond Large-Scale Production* as "the basis of Toyota's scientific approach. . . . [B]y repeating why five times, the nature of the problem as well as its (potential) solution becomes clear."[1] Ohno encouraged his team to dig into each problem that arose until they found the root cause. "Observe the production floor without preconceptions," he would advise. "Ask 'why' five times about every matter." This approach has been adopted in multiple different domains from software development to strategic management. In the strategy sphere, where one is trying to understand the true nature of a strategic challenge or opportunity, it is worth listing the perceived challenges and opportunities and then asking "why" they exist multiple times so as to move closer to uncovering and articulating root causes and key insights. With a clear statement of root causes and key insights on hand, a strategist can move toward deciding what to do about the key issues confronting the firm.

Decide

In many ways, the second D, decide, is what many of us will think of as the "heart" of strategy. Come up with the wrong decision, and no amount of brilliant analysis, implementation, or data will lead to a successful outcome. However, good decisions rely on a robust diagnosis and need a strong delivery to be implemented. In that sense, deciding is critical to good strategic management, but no more critical than diagnosing or delivering. What is tricky about the decisions strategists face is that they are often nonroutine, requiring out-of-the-box thinking and new solutions. While this makes the life of the strategist interesting, it also makes the life of the strategist complicated. In the following, we will discuss general concepts related to strategists making decisions under these challenging conditions.

Who Decides?

While it is tempting to think of organizations making decisions about future plans, we should not forget that organizations do not make decisions—people in organizations do. Cognitive heuristics and biases (blind spots) can enter into human decision-making. It is critical to be aware of these biases as even experienced decision makers (sometimes *especially* experienced decision makers) can fall victim to them. It is important to keep an awareness of all blind spots because specific situations are particularly prone to specific biases.

Key Concepts

While every decision is different, the processes by which different strategists reach decisions show a number of overlaps. The following concepts are critical to understanding what the process of deciding looks like in general. It is important to note that while these concepts may be thought of as different "phases" of the decision-making process, few decisions neatly progress linearly from start to finish. The process of decision-making is typically iterative and fluid, and so these concepts should be seen as a general overarching set of ideas that should inform the decision process, more so than a prescribed process for execution.

Generating solution alternatives. Solutions typically require creativity and innovation, as well as structure and clarity. Generating alternative options to dealing with a problem, therefore, is both a *left-brain* (structure and organization) and a *right-brain* (creativity) activity. For example, if a strategic diagnosis found that the core issue of a recent drop in sales for company A had to do with the entry of a new competitor B, a list of possible responses to B entering the market could range anywhere from lowering A's prices or changing its product positioning to stepping up A's advertising or attacking B's credibility or product. *Divergent thinking* refers to strategists brainstorming as many ideas as possible using a free-flowing, nonlinear approach. No idea is a bad idea at this time. On occasion, the search for solutions may include *recycling* or *bricolage,* meaning that ready-made ideas or solutions that were thought of before are modified to fit the particular problem. For example, company A previously having considered targeting a new market with its product but deciding not to at the time could form an alternative off-the-shelf solution when the entry of B makes the current market less profitable.

Performing an initial screen. Screening helps weed out obviously unfeasible solution alternatives. If faced with a large number of alternative options, it would be inefficient to analyze alternatives with obvious flaws to the same extent as those prime contenders that hold most promise. So, aided by the insights generated through the diagnosis stage, key actors can reduce a large number of alternatives to a smaller number of promising initiatives. Several questions can aid this selection. First, one can ask, "Does this solution align with our purpose as a company?" For example, if company A was a brewery whose purpose was to craft the most carefully brewed beer in the world, and one suggested solution to regain market share was to lower cost by replacing expensive barley malt with a cheaper corn syrup mixture, would that stand up to an initial screen? The answer is no because by doing so, the company would be choosing a path that is incongruent with its own stated purpose. A second question one can ask is, "Are there any obvious limitations or drawbacks to implementing the proposed solution?" Many prototypes never make it into actual production because of insurmountable costs or obstacles in doing so. Similarly, many strategic initiatives never make it to implementation, because there are prohibitive costs, regulations, or other forms of likely resistance stopping it. Note the use of the term *obvious* in this question. The purpose of screening is not to do in-depth research but to eliminate unpromising alternatives. A third screening question is, "Does this solution actually address the problem?" It might be surprising to learn how many proposed ideas are only loosely connected to the problem they were meant to solve. For example, while cutting costs might seem to be a good idea to company A on face value, it may not actually address the drop in sales due to the entry of company B if customers are switching to B on the basis of it having a superior product. *Hypotheses* are a limited set of proposed alternative solutions that stand up to the initial screening and are perceived to have the most promise.

Validating hypotheses. Evidence-based analysis refers to the testing of the most promising ideas through rigorous analysis. But how does one test an idea? One way to do so is by testing and validating the key *assumptions* of each idea. For example, should company A entering a new market have come out as one of the most promising ideas in our example, testing and validating this idea could involve testing the implicit assumption that the new target market would be receptive to A's product—for instance, through a survey of current customers in this new market. So, the question we can ask ourselves is, "What must be true in order for this to be the best course of action?" Intellectual honesty is key in this process of new information being collected to prove or disprove the hypotheses, as this new information may challenge previously held views. If a hypothesis is disproved, one can go back to the list of alternatives that passed the screen and choose another contender. If none of the alternatives stand the test of scrutiny, it is necessary to go back to the drawing board.

Confirming choice. Empirical research[2] indicates that managers typically use one, or a mix, of three different modes of choice between alternatives: *judgment, bargaining,* and *analysis.* A choice reached by judgment refers to individuals having decided on a solution in their own mind using procedures they might not even be able to articulate. Bargaining, in contrast, involves the eventual selection of a choice being negotiated by a group of decision makers, each of whom may have a different stake or viewpoint. A choice reached through *analysis* rests heavily on a factual evaluation of the merits of each case, after which the final decision involves either bargaining or judgment. Regardless of which of these three modes is mainly activated, the key to the phase of choosing is what psychologists refer to as *convergent thinking*: coming up with a single answer using a process that narrows the choice set through a process of elimination. In many instances, however, time pressure belies a continuing search for an optimal solution between multiple validated hypotheses. In the current, fast-paced world that we live in, oftentimes it is just not practical or feasible to continue analyzing multiple solutions in search of an optimal answer. *Satisficing* is a decision-making strategy that purports stopping the search for more alternatives when for any given solution an acceptability threshold is met.[3] A satisfying answer is one that addresses the problem or capitalizes on the opportunity to an acceptable degree and that can be arrived at with far more efficiency than an optimal solution would (if an optimal solution could even be determined at all).

Deliver

Those critical of the work of strategists often point to the lack of follow-through and tangible results. Indeed, the most elegant of strategic recommendations left unimplemented provides little demonstrable value to the organization. The final D, deliver, focuses on producing tangible positive net outcomes that help realize the business case associated with your strategic recommendations. It requires you to push beyond ideas that look good on paper and instead focus on translating those ideas into action. This is easier said than done, however, and implementing strategic recommendations typically requires substantive changes to an organization's core processes, enabling technologies, and/or human capital design. Successful strategic implementations usually span organization boundaries and lead to multiple change initiatives that take multiple years to complete. In the following, we will discuss general concepts related to strategists delivering results from their implementable solutions.

Key Concepts

While every implementation is different, the processes by which different strategists garner the support for their ideas and implement such ideas have a number of similarities. The following concepts are critical to understanding what the process of delivering looks like in broad terms. It is important to note that while these concepts may be thought of as different "phases" of the delivery, few implementations neatly progress linearly from start to finish. The implementation is typically iterative, and so these concepts should be seen as a general overarching set of ideas that guide the delivery process, more so than a prescribed sequential process for execution.

Design the recommended solution. Having decided what to do about a strategic challenge or opportunity, a key element of delivering on that decision is to integrate and fit the recommended solution into the organization. This is a design challenge. Design is the creation of a plan for the construction of an object, system, or measurable human interaction. Designs are created to achieve desirable objectives. In the case of designing a strategic solution, the objective is to integrate the specified solution within an organization such that it delivers on the specific decision that was made yet also allows the other elements of the organization to work at least as or more effectively than they did before. Therefore, strategists must recognize a business as a complex system of interrelated components while designing the solution. They must carefully account for how these complex relationships will change as a new solution is implemented. This may be facilitated by a combination of the following:

- *Systems thinking*—examining the linkages and interactions between the components that make up the entirety of a business's organization system
- *Design thinking*—using a designer's sensibility and methods to match people's needs with what is technologically feasible and what is a viable business strategy
- *Business modeling*—developing an abstract but understandable representation of how an organization creates, delivers, and captures value via all its interrelated components

There is no single or optimal approach for designing a strategic solution into an existing organization. An effective design acknowledges the nuances of the organization and the nature of the solution while attempting to create the best possible fit.

Gaining buy-in for your recommendation. Strategy is as much about garnering support for your ideas as it is about analysis. To obtain buy-in for a strategic decision, it has to be effectively communicated. A strategic decision can (and likely will) be complex and ambiguous. As a result, a strategic recommendation is only as good as the way in which it is communicated to others. Others need to understand and approve of a strategic decision if they are to act on it. And strategy needs action; otherwise, it is meaningless. When making a strategic recommendation, focus on the following:

- *Clarity.* Clarity comes from using simple terms that people understand; avoid complex jargon and technical language. Use analogies and examples where appropriate to make concepts relatable and understandable. Describe your strategies such that a fourth grader can understand what you are proposing.
- *Conciseness.* Keep strategic explanations concise. Convey your insights or perspectives in fewer rather than more words. If you ramble, you lose people. If writing, review what you write and cut out the excess. If speaking, think about what you will say and keep it short, sharp, and to the point.
- *Precision.* Use precise terms and concepts. Mentioning vague concepts and making broad sweeping statements is the antithesis to good strategic communication. If you talk about a market, be specific and precise about which market; if you mention improving a process, describe which elements of the process will be addressed and how they will be addressed. If you talk about changing customer demographics, identify the exact demographic shift; provide evidence and explain its implications.
- *Persuasion.* Being an effective strategist is as much about persuading others of the validity and relevance of your insights and choices as it is about garnering good insights and making the right choices. If you cannot persuade others of what you have decided or formulated, then it is useless. As much as you

focus on doing good analysis and making the right decisions, focus equally on how you can effectively share your insights and choices with others.

Figure 4.1 provides is a sample storyboard for a presentation that follows the guidance provided in this chapter. It assumes an inductive reasoning approach, which tends to be most suitable for senior-level audiences. The inductive approach also helps with conciseness and clarity of the message to the intended audience.

Planning the implementation. Once the key stakeholders have bought into the recommended solution, it now becomes the task

Slide -1	Slide 0	Slide 1
Table of Contents	**Background**	**Situation**
Optional - usually you can skip this and just provide a professional looking title slide	Can be useful to provide background information if the audience is not familiar with the situation. Do not use if you are presenting internally about a problem everyone is familiar with.	1. Current situation 2. Complicating factor(s) which creates tension and leads to… 3. Key question(s) Establishes scope and grounds your audience about purpose of discussion

Slide 2	Slide 3-n	Slide n+1
Answer with Quantifiable Benefit	**Rationale for your Recommendations**	**Implementation Roadmap**
1. My recommendation is X 2. The benefit of doing X is quantified in terms of either ROIC, Payback Period, or NPV	1. Usually n = 3–6 2. These slides will expose the core analysis you performed and articulate your strongest arguments in support of your hypothesis	1. Outline activities on a timeline 2. "How do we make it so?" 3. Include a Go vs. No-Go decision on your timeline

Slide n+2	Slide n+3	Appendices
Risks & Mitigations	**Call to Action!**	**Appendix Slides**
Only list risks and mitigations that are specific to the problem. High level risks that can be applicable to any problem are not helpful to outline in the presentation.	Reiterate your answer and stress the urgency to get started ASAP	Include your Logic or Hypothesis Tree here

Figure 4.1. Presentation storyboard for communicating a strategy.

of the strategist to plan for the execution steps necessary to realize real results. It is important to consider both what is to be delivered and how the delivery will be managed and monitored during that delivery. In accordance with the Project Management Institute's (PMI) guidelines for managing large-scale projects, the following components of the delivery and management plan should be considered:

Delivery plan

- *Confirm a program sponsor.* Before any change initiative starts, a sponsor with both interest and organizational influence should be identified and confirmed. This is usually the representative of the party that is funding the effort.
- *Define governance.* In addition to the organization chart, governance rules should be documented to help guide major decision-making during the execution. Typically, this planning results in the creation of a board of advisers or steering committee.
- *Create roles and responsibilities.* It is important to understand what individuals or departments will perform key activities in support of the major activities.
- *Generate work estimates.* For the defined scope, it is important to estimate the level of effort (typically in person-days) expected to complete the necessary work.
- *Schedule the work.* Using the work estimate, activities are sequenced to create a schedule that includes major milestones and deliverable due dates.
- *Determine resource needs.* It is important to identify the specific skills and resources required to complete the work prior to launching the new initiative.
- *Determine project budget.* This is an internal identification of the baseline costs, both in terms of capital expenditures (e.g., hardware or software) and labor required to complete the work.
- *Document assumptions and risks.* Document recognized assumptions that were made during planning, along with any potential risks that may jeopardize delivery.

Management plan

- *Quality assurance.* This involves an enumeration of the peer reviews or independent audits that will be performed to challenge decision-making blind spots and/or to inspect major delivery outputs.
- *Issue and risk management.* This describes the process by which you will manage issues and risks as they arise, and more specifically the escalation and resolution procedures the execution team will abide by.
- *Measurement.* This involves identification of the major performance metrics and how they will be measured to chart success and ultimately allow the strategist to claim victory.
- *Communication.* Given the array of stakeholders and their varied interests, it is important to consider the manner and frequency of how you will communicate with each of these stakeholders.

Monitoring the execution. Typically, strategists don't consider execution the core of their job function, and while they are never likely to play a prominent role in implementation activities, there are a few important activities strategists can engage in to ensure the organizational benefits outlined in the recommendation are realized. Provided next are guidelines for these activities:

- *Monitor the business case closely.* To develop the original business case, which expresses the organization's required investment and expected benefits of implementing the strategy, a number of assumptions must be made. After all, a business case is in fact some forecast of future performance. During the execution, it becomes the strategist's primary role to monitor the actual performance against these forecasted assumptions. Moreover, it becomes important to remind the delivery team of the intended outcomes of their work to ensure that choices made during implementation align with these expected results.
- *Develop milestones and contingency plans.* As discussed earlier in this chapter, strategic recommendations often lead to multiyear,

multiproject implementation efforts. During the journey, it becomes important to identify key milestones for two significant reasons. First, breaking up the monotony of a long, perhaps tiresome implementation affords opportunities to celebrate success along the way. In turn, this can help keep motivation levels high and ensure organizational commitment to the process. Second, and perhaps more important, it provides the strategist an opportunity to identify contingency plans that can be put in place along the way that allow the organization to gracefully exit the strategy or change course without eroding benefits previously realized. Very rarely do decision makers "buy" the entire strategic recommendation all at once upfront. Instead, astute strategists plan for and present their recommendations in more manageable phases or steps. This helps minimize the risk associated with the recommendation and in turn eases its initial acceptance.

- *Encourage continuous improvement.* Finally, strategists, just like all employees, should contribute to the organization by encouraging the need for continuous improvement during the implementation. This includes refining not only the implementation plan and tactics but also the strategic recommendation and/or its intended outcomes. Industries are moving at an increasingly brisk pace, and often the facts and beliefs held at the time the strategic recommendation was developed become outdated or no longer true. Wise strategists will recognize this and are not afraid to change course based on a refresh of these new facts and beliefs in an effort to refine and improve the recommendation and/or its subsequent implementation.

PART II
TOOLS

5

A Strategy Toolbox

The process of *diagnosing* strategic issues or opportunities, *deciding* what to do about them, and taking action to *deliver* on such decisions is facilitated, enhanced, and streamlined with a collection of concepts, frameworks, and theories—what we broadly refer to as *tools*—that help a strategist more clearly think about, understand, and interpret important issues at hand and decide what to do about them.

Clayton Christensen, the well-renowned Harvard Business School professor, described his approach to dealing with diverse business challenges and opportunities across a range of different industries and organizations as follows:

> As an academic I'm asked hundreds of times a year to offer opinions on specific business challenges in industries or organizations in which I have no special knowledge, yet I am able to provide insight because there is a toolbox full of theories (including concepts and frameworks) that teach me not what to think, but rather how to think. Good theory is the best way I know to frame problems in such way that we ask the right questions to get us to the most useful answers. Embracing theory is not to mire ourselves in academic minutia, but quite the opposite: to focus on the supremely practical question of what causes what (and what to do about it). Theory has a voice, but no agenda. Theory does not change its mind. It does apply to some companies or people and not to others. Theories are not right or wrong. They provide accurate predictions (or explanations) given the circumstances you're in.[1]

Effective managers are expected to develop, refine, and use a conceptual toolbox made up of tools (concepts, frameworks, and theories) that enable them to make sense of and act on challenging situations and complex opportunities. Such a conceptual toolbox takes time to develop, and learning *when* and *how* to use the tools in one's toolbox is nuanced, but critically important. Using a tool at the wrong time or in the wrong way can lead to disastrous results.

In this section we provide the fundamental tools that form the foundation of a strategist's toolbox. This is by no means an exhaustive set of tools. It is a basic set of tools that most managers are expected to know and effectively apply. These tools are the equivalent of a hammer, screwdriver, chisel, drill, pencil, and tape measure in a more traditional toolbox. And as carpenters become more experienced and deal with more challenging projects, they may expand their tools, but they will still depend heavily on the basic fundamental tools, just as managers will repeatedly draw on the tools described in this section even as they use more sophisticated analytical approaches and options. The language associated with the tools described in this section often becomes part of the vernacular used in boardrooms and among executives and senior managers. So these tools not only provide new ways of seeing but also facilitate communication in the upper echelons of the business world.

Many of the tools that we introduce in this section are used across different elements of the strategy process: diagnose, decide, and deliver. Because of their fundamental nature, they are not used in only one scenario for one type of issue. Similar to a hammer that one might use for knocking in nails, tapping joints together, or extracting nails across various different phases of a woodworking or do-it-yourself project, the tools described in this section may apply across a variety of scenarios and get used for various purposes. Table 5.1 highlights the tools presented in this book, with a key to suggest where the tool might be more or less relevant.

Next, we introduce and explain each of these tools. To do so we describe the overall purpose of the tool, the core idea, and the theory

Table 5.1 The Basic Tools in a Strategy Toolbox

	Diagnose	Decide	Deliver
STEEP	●	○	
Five forces	●	○	
Competitor analysis	●	○	
VRIO	●	○	
Financial performance analysis	●		○
SWOT	●	○	
Root-cause analysis	●	○	
S-curve	○	●	
Value chain analysis	○	●	
Hypothesis testing	○	●	
Segmentation analysis	○	●	
Vertical integration	○	●	
Market penetration	○	●	○
Business model canvas	○	○	●
Balanced scorecard	○	○	●

Key	
●	= Most prevalent use
◐	= High likelihood of also being valuable
○	= May also have benefit/application

underpinning the tool. We also represent each tool in a graphical format and lay out the general process for using the tool in a strategic scenario. We highlight the value created by each tool, as well as its risks and limitations, and provide some additional references that can deepen the reader's understanding of the tool.

6
STEEP

Purpose and Objective

The purpose of a macro-environmental (STEEP) analysis is to capture and interpret what is happening (and what is likely to happen) in the environment in which a business operates. STEEP stands for social, technical, economic, ecological, and political and does not prioritize one environmental factor over another. It provides a structured way to account for the trends, forces, and changes beyond the boundaries of the firm, which may impact the operations and markets of the firm.

Underlying Theory

The STEEP framework has been around for a number of decades and has gained widespread recognition. Rather than being intrinsically tied to one distinct theoretical perspective, STEEP analysis, in its various forms, has touchpoints with multiple strands of business and management research that are broadly interested in understanding, monitoring, and shaping the organizational environment. As such, STEEP has conceptual connections to theories that place a heavy emphasis on the environment like resource dependence theory[1] and population ecology.[2] However, such relations are relatively loose and STEEP analysis should mainly be viewed as a broad, encompassing heuristic for strategically classifying and monitoring the *organizational environment*—that is, "the broad set of forces emanating or operating from outside the organization that can affect its competitive performance."[3]

A central assumption in theories of the organizational environment is that organizational performance and survival depend, at least in part, on an organizational environment that can withhold or supply critical resources on which organizations depend. Pfeffer and Salancik defined *environmental dependence* as a combination of the importance of a resource to the organization and the number of sources from which the resource is available, as well as the number, variety, and relative power of organizations competing for the resource.[4]

The earliest reference to STEEP analysis specifically is a study by Francis J. Aguilar that dates back to 1967, who discussed "ETPS" as a taxonomy of the environment: economic, technical, political, and social.[5] Since then, authors have jumbled these letters into several orderings (not necessarily related to any specific order of importance) and added "ecological" as a separate factor in its own right, leading to the common use of the term *STEEP*.

The environment can be conceptually divided into three levels: *internal environment* (forces inside the organization), *operating environment* (meso-level forces that are external to the organization but that have direct and relatively immediate relationships with the organization, like customers, suppliers, competitors, and strategic partners), and the *general environment* (broad, macro-level forces external to the organization, which have more long-term influences and are generally beyond the control of the organization). STEEP factors are generally at play at the level of the general environment.[6]

Core Idea

Macro-environmental (STEEP) analysis acts as a checklist for evaluating the trends, forces, and changes beyond the boundaries of the firm that may create opportunities or threats for a firm or industry. Each letter in the STEEP acronym accounts for a major macro-environmental factor that may impact a business or industry, now or in the future. These macro-environmental factors are as follows: (1) sociocultural factors, (2) technological factors,

(3) economic factors, (4) ecological factors, and (5) political and legal factors. By covering each of these major factors in a macro-environmental analysis, a strategist can be somewhat confident that the majority of major macro-environmental issues that may impact the strategy and performance of a firm have been considered. Table 6.1 provides a summary of the macro-environmental factors that are considered in a STEEP analysis.

Depiction

Figure 6.1 provides a visual depiction of the key macro-environmental factors in a STEEP analysis in relation to an industry and a firm.

Process

1. For each major macro-economic factor (sociocultural, techno-logical, economic, ecological, and political/legal) spend time brainstorming and researching major trends, forces, and changes.
2. Identify and describe the most salient trends, forces, and changes under each factor. Collect extra data on each salient trend, force, or change, if necessary.
3. Examine salient trends, forces, and changes for each factor alongside one another. Identify interconnections and dependencies between them.
4. Forecast future directions and implications for each salient trend, force, or change.
5. Derive implications for the strategy of the firm from each salient trend, force, or change identified.

Table 6.1 Macro-Environmental Factors in a STEEP Analysis

Factors	Description	Considerations
Sociocultural factors	Sociocultural factors capture societies' cultures, norms, beliefs, and behaviors, as well as demographic shifts in population distribution.	• Ideological issues and concerns • Lifestyle and fashion trends • Population growth and segmentation • Age distribution • Media views and influence
Technological factors	Technological factors account for technology changes and trajectories, including the emergence of new technologies that may disrupt a firm or industry.	• Technology maturity • Emergent technology developments • Pace of technological change • Research funding and focus • Licensing and patenting norms and regulations
Economic factors	Economic factors account for shifts in economic indicators and trends and the impact of those indicators and trends on a firm and industry.	• Gross domestic product growth rates • Interest rates • Employment levels • Price stability (inflation and deflation) • Currency exchange rates • Income distribution
Ecological factors	Ecological factors concern broad environmental issues pertaining to the natural environment, global warming, and sustainable economic growth.	• Consumer preferences and demands for sustainable products and services • Environmental regulation and incentives • Access to sustainable resources (e.g., natural resources)
Political and legal factors	Political and legal factors account for the processes and actions of government and for changes in relevant laws, regulations, policies, and incentives.	• Industry laws and regulations • Political party policies and power distribution • Ability to influence political decisions • Voting rates and trends • Power and focus of regulatory agencies

Figure 6.1. STEEP tool to analyze factors in the external environment.

Insight or Value Created

A macro-environmental (STEEP) analysis provides perspective and insight on significant environmental issues that may have impacted a firm's level of competitiveness in the past and/or may impact competitiveness in the future. As such, it may serve as a key input into a strategic diagnosis and discussion.

The activity prompts managers to think about issues that exist beyond a firm's boundaries and outside its immediate concerns and activities. It provides a big-picture perspective for evaluating what has happened and what is likely to happen with a firm in relation to its environment.

Risks and Limitations

A macro-environmental (STEEP) analysis is highly dependent on a manager's interpretation of salient trends, forces, and changes. It helps managers consider trends, forces, and changes under different major categories but does not really provide a way for them to assess which issues have had, or will have, the most significant impact on the business. Different managers may interpret different issues under each of the major STEEP factors very differently.

A macro-environmental (STEEP) analysis requires a long-term orientation, yet many managers are assessed on short-term performance. Therefore, some managers may feel that the issues that arise from a STEEP analysis will take too long to affect the performance of a firm and hence are beyond the scope of issues they wish to consider as a means to impact firm performance.

Case Illustration: Japan Tobacco International

Context

In 2010, Japan Tobacco International (JTI) was the world's third-largest tobacco company, with a global market share of 11% and a market capitalization of approximately $32 billion. The company manufactures and markets internationally recognized brands across the globe, including three of the top five worldwide cigarette brands: Winston, the fastest-growing brand worldwide; Camel, the originator of American Blend; and Mild Seven, the global leader in charcoal filter cigarettes.

JTI had been experiencing a slow yet observable decline in sales domestically in Japan since the turn of the century. To confirm their suspicions and seek clarity on casual factors, JTI decided to consult the Japan Smoking Rate Survey, a survey that has been carried out annually since 1965. The survey, conducted in May of 2009, showed that 24.9% of Japanese adults were smokers, down from 25.7% the year prior. A breakdown by gender of the results of the survey is provided in Table 6.2, and Table 6.3 shows Japanese smoking trends over time.

Further analysis of the survey results revealed that the contributing factors for this decline included an increased emphasis on health,

Table 6.2 Percentage of Japanese Smokers by Age as of May 2009

Gender	Age				
	20–29	30–39	40–49	50–59	60+
Men	17.8%	15.9%	16.1%	16.9%	33.4%
Women	11.7%	17.5%	16.9%	17.6%	36.3%
Total	14.8%	16.7%	16.5%	17.2%	34.8%

Table 6.3 Japanese Smoking Trend: 2008 Versus 2009

	2008 (in Millions)	2009 (in Millions)	Change (in Millions)	% Change
Men	39.5	38.9	−0.6	−1.52
Women	12.9	11.9	−1.0	−7.75
Total	52.4	50.8	−1.6	−3.05

more stringent national smoking regulations, and the introduction of vending machines with age verification functions in major urban areas throughout the country.

Analyzing the Macro-Environment Trends

With these trends in the Japanese domestic market, it became imperative for JTI to analyze the macro-environment and make a decision regarding its presence both at home and abroad. To illustrate the process of conducting a macro-environmental analysis, let us go through the steps described earlier in the chapter and apply them to JTI.

Step 1: For each major macro-economic factor (sociocultural, technological, economic, ecological, political/legal) spend time brainstorming and researching major trends, forces, and changes. The key to identifying major trends and market forces impacting JTI is to not make this is a transactional, one-time task. Rather, organizational leaders should be continuing to scan the macro-environment and refreshing each factor by virtue of simply being well read. Common sources for staying abreast of changes include regular review of popular press magazines and newspapers (e.g., *Fortune, Wall Street Journal, The Economist*), subscribing to industry journals (e.g., *Cigar Aficionado, Tobacco Business Magazine*), and attending industry conferences (e.g., International Premium Cigar and Pipe Retailers Annual Convention, World Conference on Tobacco and Health).

Step 2: Identify and describe the most salient trends, forces, and changes under each factor. Collect extra data on each salient trend, force, or change, if necessary. Using resources similar to those described earlier, the following salient trends were identified as being particularly impactful to JTI's business in 2009:

Social
- Aging Japanese population that is shrinking in total size (–)
- Population becoming more health conscious (–)

Technological
- Tobacco alternatives and smokeless substitutes on the rise (–)
- Research and development in pharmaceuticals business on the rise (+)
- Age verification on vending machines in major urban centers (–)

Environmental
- Forest preservation becoming a larger legislative priority in Japan (–)

Economic
- Pending tax increases on cigarettes (–)

Political
- Democratic Party of Japan (DPJ) wants to reduce smoking rates (–)
- DPJ currently mandates that JTI purchase all its tobacco leaf from locally sourced growers in Japan (–)

Step 3: Examine salient trends, forces, and changes for each factor alongside one another. Identify interconnections and dependencies between them. Through the analysis described previously, it becomes clear that the company faced significant challenges by continuing to rely on its domestic market as a source of growth. Not only was the population of Japan shrinking in size, but also there were both political pressures and technological advances that would make growth in the market an unrealistic goal going forward. In particular, the DPJ had been transparent in their desire to reduce smoking rates among the Japanese population and as a result had recently mandated that all vending machines dispensing tobacco products be equipped with age verification devices. This barrier to increasing sales was accompanied by mandated increases in JTI's raw material costs as well. The DPJ had also enacted a policy that would require JTI, as well as its competitors, to source tobacco leaf from local growers in Japan. This law effectively increased JTI's input costs virtually overnight, as Japanese leaves were four times more expensive than imported tobacco.

Step 4: Forecast future directions and implications for each salient trend, force, or change. Downward pressure on sales combined with increases in the costs of goods sold meant lasting margin erosion that made continued reliance on the domestic market for growth an unrealistic strategy going forward.

Step 5: Derive implications for the strategy of the firm from each salient trend, force, or change identified. JTI made the decision to fortify its core business in Japan by maintaining its market share while simultaneously focusing on building a more cost-efficient operating structure. To do this, JTI closed two Japanese domestic tobacco factories at the end of March 2010 as part of its bold efforts to build an optimum operating structure. The factory closures allowed JTI to stabilize profits in the domestic market. By the end of 2011, JTI had managed to increase earnings before interest, tax, depreciation, and amortization (EBITDA) by approximately 6 billion yen despite modest declines in domestic sales. Simultaneously, JTI turned its attention to its international business to achieve sustainable top-line growth by investing in initiatives to expand its product portfolio and build brand equity overseas. By the end of 2010, international sales volume totaled 435 billion cigarettes, significantly outpacing domestic sales of 152 billion cigarettes.

7
Five Forces

Purpose and Objective

A five-forces analysis provides a basis to evaluate and understand an industry and its broad set of participants including suppliers, customers, and competitors. It provides a means for managers and practitioners to assess the major factors impacting an industry's profit potential and may help highlight ways that a firm may increase its profit potential relative to the other industry participants.

Underlying Theory

Five-forces analysis was developed and popularized by Michael Porter, who in 1979 wrote a ground-breaking article in the *Harvard Business Review* entitled "How Competitive Forces Shape Strategy,"[1] which set forth the idea that an awareness of five competitive forces (the threat of new entrants, the bargaining power of customers, the bargaining power of suppliers, the threat of substitute products or services, and the jockeying among current contestants) can help companies stake out superior competitive positions. As Porter noted:

> Industry structure, as manifested in the strength of the five competitive forces, determines the industry's long-run profit potential because it determines how the economic value created by the industry is divided—how much is retained by companies in the industry versus bargained away by customers and suppliers, limited by substitutes, or constrained by potential new entrants. By considering all five forces, a strategist keeps overall structure in mind instead of gravitating to any one

element. In addition, the strategist's attention remains focused on structural conditions rather than on fleeting factors. It is especially important to avoid the common pitfall of mistaking certain visible attributes of an industry for its underlying structure.[2]

The novelty of Porter's work at the time, fueled by insights derived from industrial economics, was in seeing competition as being more than merely the manifestation of other firms vying for the same market. Rather, competition for profits includes the competitive forces that stem from customers, suppliers, potential entrants, and substitute products.

Porter's central assumption is that the essence of strategy formulation lies in coping with competition. Recalling STEEP analysis's main concern with an organization's general environment, five-forces analysis is mainly concerned with the operating environment.

Despite (or perhaps because of) its prevalence, five-forces analysis has received its share of criticism as well—for supposedly being *static* (i.e., the fact that five forces is typically not used to track industry evolution but rather take snapshots of reality at distinct points in time); for underrepresenting the *interrelationships* among buyers, competitors, and suppliers; and for being *deterministic and general* in the sense that all industries are assumed to basically function in the same way in terms of the underlying drivers of profitability and how they relate to one another.

Core Idea

Five distinct forces affect industry profitability: (1) the negotiating power of suppliers, (2) the negotiating power of buyers, (3) the level of rivalry between competitors in that industry, (4) the threat of new entrants into the industry (i.e., the extent to which there are barriers to entry to get into the industry), and (5) the threat of substitute products (i.e., the extent to which buyers may substitute the industry's products with other products if they don't like what the industry is offering). These five forces impact industry profitability as follows:

- The greater the negotiating power of suppliers, the more influence they have to increase prices and extract profits, and the lower the profitability of the industry.
- The greater the negotiating power of buyers, the more influence they have to negotiate lower prices and hence depress profits in the industry.
- The higher the level of rivalry among competitors in the industry, the more they will be forced to lower prices or provide extra value to continue to attract customers, and the lower the overall profitability of the industry.
- The greater the threat of new entrants into the industry (i.e., the lower the entry barriers to get into the industry), the higher the likelihood that new entrants will enter to capture profits, and the lower the profitability of the industry.
- The greater the threat of substitute products, the higher the likelihood that buyers will switch their preferences if industry product prices get too high, thus lowering the profitability of the industry.

Some of the factors that impact the forces in a five-forces analysis are depicted in Table 7.1.

Depiction

The five forces impacting industry profitability are depicted in Figure 7.1.[3]

Process

The process for conducting a five forces analysis is as follows:[4]

Table 7.1 Factors Impacting the Five Forces

Force	This Force Increases with the Following*
Negotiating power of suppliers	• High supplier concentration (i.e., few suppliers) • High differentiation of inputs • High switching costs to different suppliers • Lack of substitute inputs • High threats of forward integration by suppliers
Negotiating power of buyers	• High buyer volumes • Low buyer switching costs • Increased information available to buyers • High seller dependence on buyers (i.e., seller dependence on a few customers) • High threat of backward integration by buyers • Low levels of product differentiation • Substitute products available to buyers
Level of rivalry between competitors	• High exit barriers in the industry • Low levels of industry concentration • High fixed costs to operate • Low industry growth • Overcapacity in the industry • Low product differences • Low switching costs for buyers
Threat of new entrants	• Low economies of scale within the industry • Low product differentiation and/or brand equity • Low capital requirements • Low switching costs for buyers • Easy access to distribution channels • No government policy restricting industry • Easy access to necessary inputs • Limited learning curve benefits for incumbents • Limited expected retaliation from incumbents • Limited patent and trademark protection
Threat of substitute products	• Low switching costs • High buyer inclination to substitute • Low price-performance tradeoff • Easy ability to substitute

* Adapted from Porter, M. *Competitive Advantage: Creating and Sustaining Superior Performance.* (New York, NY: Free Press, 1985).

1. Define the relevant industry by both its product scope and geographic scope.
2. Identify the players constituting each of the five forces; where appropriate, segment them into groups.

Figure 7.1. Five-forces tool to analyze industry profitability.

3. Assess the underlying drivers of each force. *Which are strong? Which are weak? Why?*
4. Step back and assess the overall industry structure. *Which forces control profitability? Which firms are substantially more profitable than industry averages? Why?*
5. Analyze recent and likely future changes for each force. *How are they trending? What might happen in the future?*
6. How can a firm position itself in relation to the five forces? *Is there a position where the forces are weakest? Is it possible to exploit industry change? Can the industry be reshaped to favor a firm?*

Insight or Value Created

A five-forces analysis highlights that firms are in a competition for profits, not just with rivals, but also with other industry participants. Business competition is the struggle of capturing the value that an industry creates.

Companies compete for profits with their direct rivals and also with other industry participants including customers, suppliers, potential new entrants, and makers of substitutes.

The collective strength of the five forces determines the average profitability of the industry through their impact on prices, costs, and the investment required to compete. A good strategy produces profits better than the industry average by leveraging the forces in a firm's favor.

Using five-forces analysis simply to declare that an industry is attractive or unattractive misses its full power as a tool. Because industry structure can "explain" the income statements and balance sheets of firms in an industry, insights gained therefrom can strongly inform decisions about where and how to compete.

Industry structure is dynamic, not static. Five-forces analysis can help anticipate and exploit structural change.[5]

Risks and Limitations

Critics of the five-forces model point out that it underestimates the capabilities, resources, and core competencies of a firm. These may serve as long-term sources of competitive advantage but are somewhat overlooked in the five-forces analysis.

The model is designed to analyze individual business unit strategies within an industry. Hence, it can overlook synergies and interdependencies among a corporation's various business units.

Some critics suggest that the five-forces model does not adequately account for social, political, and technological factors impacting a business. It may account for some such factors indirectly, but social, political, and technological factors are central to a firm's strategy in the current environment.

A risk of making changes to industry structure to benefit a firm is that other firms may also benefit significantly from a firm's efforts to adapt to industry structure. A company may allocate resources to shift industry structure in a particular way (e.g., erect barriers to entry) but then fail to derive unique benefit because all other firms in the industry are subject to the same changes (e.g., lobbying for a particular beneficial government regulation or deregulation would benefit all industry members).

Case Illustration: Harley-Davidson

Context

In the second half of 2015, Harley-Davidson Inc., the Milwaukee-based manufacturer and seller of distinctive and customizable motorcycles, started facing challenges in the United States and took a big hit in profitability. Over the course of 2016 to 2018, shipments to dealers were down, retail sales dipped, and plants were closed. Historically, Harley-Davidson's mission was to design and manufacture premium, heavyweight motorcycles for the U.S. market; "A big bike, lots of chrome, almost 1700cc, and that classic, easy riding style."[6] Analysts attempted to diagnose what the possible issues underlying these negative trends might be. One pertinent question that arose was whether the industry segment Harley was playing in was actually still attractive and profitable.

Assessing the Profitability of the Heavyweight Motorcycle Industry

Five-forces analysis is well suited to help answer whether a given industry segment is still profitable. To illustrate the process of conducting five-forces analysis, let us go through the steps described earlier in this chapter and apply them to Harley-Davidson, with an emphasis on the trends as they were occurring over the 2015–2018 period.

Step 1: Define the relevant industry by both its product scope and geographic scope. In this first step, the problem faced by the company should be the leading factor defining the relevant product scope and geographic scope. In this case, let us focus our main attention on the heavyweight motorcycle market (which is a recreational, customer discretionary market segment) both in the United States and globally, as this is the traditional mainstay of Harley's market positioning.

Step 2: Identify the players constituting each of the five forces. In the case of Harley-Davidson, the five forces consist of the following players:

- *Suppliers.* According to Harley's own comments on its supply chain, suppliers are used to buy both raw materials (steel and aluminum castings, forgings, and steel sheets and bars, mostly) and motorcycle components (including electronic fuel injection systems, batteries, certain wheels, tires, seats, and electrical components and instruments). At a high level, suppliers to Harley-Davidson are both major corporations like Alcoa Corp., U.S. Steel Corp., 3M, and Honda and many smaller companies used for specialized parts.[7]
- *Buyers.* Harley-Davidson's principal buyers of its heavyweight machines were a quite specific customer segment: American middle-aged men with disposable income.[8]
- *Competitors.* Harley-Davidson's main competitors were mainly large, and sometimes diversified, other sellers of heavyweight motorcycles, including Honda, Suzuki, Yamaha, Ducati, Kawasaki, and BMW.[9]
- *New entrants.* Immediate new entrants to the heavyweight motorcycle industry that would be able to produce at a scale similar to Harley-Davidson were not envisioned, given the high barriers to entry and dwindling buyer volume.
- *Substitute products.* As a discretionary and luxury product, Harley-Davidson's heavyweight motorcycles faced several possible substitute products. As a method to get from A to B, substitute products included cars, public transport, and scooters, and from the perspective of lifestyle and the comradery of riding as a group, one could even envision road bicycles. The main substitute products, however, to Harley's main focus on large, heavyweight motorcycles were smaller, less expensive, more

lightweight, and more versatile and eco-friendly sport bikes produced for a younger, international demographic.

Step 3: Assess the underlying drivers of each force. This is a critical step in which we determine, based on our knowledge of the case and analysis of relevant data, how strong each force is. In our assessment of the information directly available to us, this would look as follows:

- *Negotiating power of suppliers.* Three important factors determined the power of suppliers to Harley-Davidson. First, Harley operated many stages of the production of a motorcycle itself, leaving quite a few options for sourcing many of the relatively general inputs that Harley requires. Second, Harley-Davidson maintained and reinforced long-term relationships with suppliers, which protect the company against opportunistic behavior on the part of suppliers. Third, the threat of forward integration by suppliers was quite limited. For these reasons, we assess the negotiating power of suppliers as being relatively low.
- *Negotiating power of buyers.* Several important trends can be observed when looking at the negotiating power of buyers. First, the buyer volume for Harley's main segment was no longer growing. U.S. baby boomers, Harley's main segment for heavyweight bikes, were aging, and the average Harley rider's age had inched up to almost fifty.[10] In addition, the switching cost for buyers away from Harley-Davidson and to a competitor were relatively low. Buyers were also increasingly well informed of the motorcycles on the market, their pricing, and their quality and performance. For these reasons, we rate the negotiating power of buyers as high, and further increasing.
- *Level of rivalry among competitors.* Harley faced some formidable competitors, including large, diversified firms like BMW and Honda that could ride out lows in the motorcycle industry better than Harley. Low industry growth over the 2012–2017 period served to increase the level of rivalry, as did the relatively low switching costs for buyers. For these reasons, we assess the level of rivalry among competitors to be high.

- *Threat of new entrants.* Motorcycle manufacturing is, at least for the mass market, a game of scale, with high capital requirements and high requirements for distribution channels. Moreover, in the case of Harley-Davidson, it is important to point out that Harley owners bought more than a motorcycle; they also bought a lifestyle.[11] As such, we would assess the strength of new entrants, particularly for the heavyweight market as is our focus here, to be low in this case.
- *Threat of substitute products.* The threat of substitute products is high. Apart from the really distinct methods of transportation that we outlined, Harley's heavyweight motorcycles can, and in fact at the time were, being substituted by smaller, more agile, less expensive, and more eco-friendly alternatives sold in the international market to a younger audience.

Step 4: Step back and assess the overall industry structure. Looking at the overall industry structure, the most salient drivers of profitability were the high power of buyers, including the dwindling demographic that was Harley's key customer segment, and the threat of competition and substitution by competitors producing a different type of bike. The firms that had been particularly successful were firms like BMW and Ducati in Europe, which focused on engineering precision and racing performance, and the "big four" companies from Japan (Honda, Kawasaki, Suzuki, and Yamaha), which focused on smaller, less expensive, lighter-weight motorcycles that were attracting a younger and more diverse customer segment.[12]

Step 5: Analyze recent and likely future changes for each force. Let us focus on the key trends and likely changes in the dimensions that we revealed in the previous step. As for buyers and Harley-Davidson's key product focus and market segment, the outlook was grim. As we pointed out, U.S. baby boomers were and are aging, and those in that population wanting to buy a big, heavyweight machine would quite likely already have done so. In fact, confronted with younger, more price-sensitive buyers hesitant to really embrace the brand,[13] Harley-Davidson needed to make some important strategic changes. In addition, the substitute products offered by competing firms were expected to be a better match with the changing market demographic, which going forward was also likely to include more women riding motorcycles, serving to only exacerbate the gap between Harley-Davidson and its main competition.

Step 6: How can a firm position itself in relation to the five forces? Overall it seems that Harley-Davidson was facing a tough industry segment, which meant profitability was only projected to deteriorate as the main segment aged, and competitors continued to offer products better aligned with changing buyer preferences. This five-forces analysis shows the need for a strategic repositioning by Harley-Davidson, which would have to include appealing to a younger, global new buyer by offering distinctive new products more aligned with their wishes, even while not compromising Harley's stable supplier network and iconic brand.

In conclusion, five-forces analysis tells us that Harley-Davidson's strategic positioning was less than optimal, as it was active in a heavyweight motorcycle segment that was slowly becoming less profitable. It should be no wonder that Harley-Davidson would soon embark on an ambitious new strategy to build the next generation of riders. We will return to Harley-Davidson in our chapters on VRIO analysis (Chapter 9) and segmentation analysis (Chapter 16) to further flesh out the strategic issues at play and to follow up on what that ambitious new strategy entailed.

8

Competitor Analysis

Purpose and Objective

The purpose of a competitor analysis is to provide managers and practitioners with a complete picture of the competitive landscape confronting a firm. This includes an assessment of the strengths and weaknesses of current and future competitors. It is deceptively simple and only one part of a more robust strategic analysis, yet a competitor analysis is an indispensable tool in a strategist's toolkit. A superior knowledge of competitors provides a firm with a competitive advantage.

Underlying Theory

While a basic, intuitive awareness of competition has always been integral to organizing for profit, the systematic framework for competitor analysis that we know today was introduced and developed by Michael Porter in two influential books in the 1980s.[1,2] Porter's essential premise was that competitor analysis should be a central component of strategy because *customer value* is always defined relative to rival offerings.[3] Hence, superior competitive positions can only be obtained and maintained if one has detailed knowledge of one's competitors.

One of the underlying ideas behind competitor analysis is the concept of proactive *competitor profiling*, in terms of asking what drives the competitor, how the competitor is currently competing, what assumptions the competitor holds about itself and the market, and what the competitor's main capabilities and weaknesses are.

This sort of proactive competitor profiling has three advantages:[4] (1) it can reveal strategic weaknesses in competitors that the firm can exploit, (2) it can reveal insights about likely strategic responses by competitors to planned initiatives, and (3) it can make the firm more agile in terms of being able to anticipate future strategic moves by competitors.

Core Idea

The core idea behind a competitor analysis is to use a systematic approach to (1) identify current and future competitive rivals to a firm, (2) assess the strengths and weaknesses of current and future competitive rivals, (3) determine a match between a competitor's strategies and capabilities, (4) analyze the future plans and intentions of competitive rivals, and (5) predict a competitor's reaction to competitive initiatives launched by a firm.

A competitor analysis uses past and current information about competitors to make estimates and predictions. It provides a basis to predict future strategic moves by competitors in response to a firm's strategy and outlines gaps and opportunities within a competitive landscape. To do this, a competitor analysis may assess five aspects of a competitor as summarized in Table 8.1.

Depiction

The key considerations in a competitor analysis are depicted in Figure 8.1.[5] This figure shows how one can break down a competitor analysis into the competitor's drivers and its capabilities and resources.

Process

1. Identify current and future competitors.

Table 8.1 Key Aspects of a Competitor Analysis

Focus Area	Issues	Key Question
Objectives	Competitor's future goals and philosophies	What are management's drivers?
Assumptions	Competitor's management assumptions	What assumptions does management have about themselves, their firm, the industry, and other salient trends, forces, and changes?
Strategies	Competitor's current strategies	How is the competitor currently competing?
Capabilities and Resources	Competitor's current capabilities	What are the current strengths and weaknesses of the competitor?
Response	Competitor's likely response	What is the competitor's real (versus claimed) focus? What likely moves or shifts will the competitor make? Where are the competitor's blind spots or false assumptions? What will the competitor's likely response be to market initiatives?

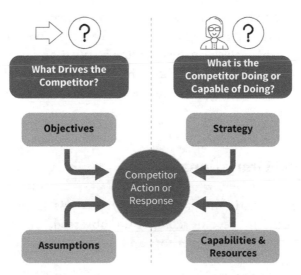

Figure 8.1. Competitor analysis tool to assess direct competitors.

2. Gather intelligence on competitors. Source publicly available materials (e.g., analyst reports, websites, financial reports and other Securities and Exchange Commission filings, media coverage, interviews with managers, press releases, etc.). Also consider becoming a customer of competitors by buying their products or services.
3. Consolidate, analyze, and organize information. Information may be organized in a matrix, grid, or spider diagram.
4. Summarize insights from competitor analysis, including opportunities, gaps, and threats stemming from the analysis.
5. Derive strategic implications for the focal firm.
6. Continue to monitor competitors over time.

Insight or Value Created

A competitor analysis can provide a clear picture of the competitive landscape, which can then be used by managers or practitioners to inform business decisions and strategic choices.

It may enable a firm to identify underserved areas in a market, as well as saturated or overserved areas in a market, so that the opportunities and threats within a market become more evident.

A competitor analysis can help create a competitor-conscious culture within an organization, prompting managers and employees to be aware of and reactive to the competitive environment in which a firm operates.

Risks and Limitations

The primary criticism of competitor analysis is that it may prompt firms to become competitor obsessed, meaning they focus excessively on competitors and lose touch with customers and markets.

It may blind a company to new and innovative approaches and technologies that emerge from outside a firm's competitor set.

Reliance on competitor analysis may result in firms instituting a copycat approach to strategy development, in which competitors' strategies are the source of new ideas, rather than developing new ideas internally or seeking new ideas from other industries and markets.

Case Illustration: Netflix

Context

To illustrate how to do a competitor analysis, let us look at Netflix. In 2018, the global subscription service for streaming movies and TV shows had more than 117 million streaming memberships in over 190 countries.[6] Netflix had disrupted the world market for entertainment video. At the time, its explosive growth had started to attract some formidable competition. Was the company in a position to stave off the threat these new competitors posed?

Mapping Netflix's Competitors

Step 1: Identify current and future competitors. Netflix's main market was the fast-changing market for entertainment video. To identify current competitors, the obvious path is to look at companies with a similar position in the value chain, which offer a similar product. Doing so for Netflix in 2018 would identify Amazon Prime Video and Hulu as two obvious competitors for Netflix.

Possible future competitors are trickier to identify, but to do so one can look for companies that could satisfy similar customer needs, irrespective of whether they currently operate a competing product. Two companies that come to mind are Disney (which was technically higher up in the value chain on the production side but could forward integrate) and Apple (which was technically lower in the value chain on the end-user consumption side but could backward integrate). Neither of these companies had a streaming service at the time (though Disney reportedly was planning to launch one). For the sake of illustrating the tool, let us focus our analysis on these four current and relatively likely future competitors, keeping in mind that a full list of current and future competitors would be much more comprehensive than this.

Step 2: Gather intelligence on competitors. In step 2, we gather data on these competitors. In this case, we have the advantage of dealing with large, public companies on which a lot of publicly available data can be sourced. This isn't always the case though. The authors once worked with a local pizza restaurant that wanted to grow and diversify its business. In the process, we found out the owner conducted competitor analysis on its local competitors by ordering pizzas from them at regular intervals, interviewing staff that had previously worked there, and regularly patrolling their parking lots! In the case of Netflix, however, obtaining relevant data about its main competitors is relatively straightforward.

Step 3: Consolidate, analyze, and organize information. Let us summarize the data we collected in step 2 and present them at a relatively high level as follows:

- *Amazon Prime Video.* As of 2012, Amazon had started offering its video streaming service as a benefit to an Amazon Prime membership. In April 2018, Amazon had over 100 million Amazon Prime members globally.[7] Apart from thousands of movies and series, Prime Video contained original content (Prime Originals) and NFL Thursday Night Football. Two key distinguishing features of this competitor are first, that Amazon has really, really deep pockets (its reported 2018 budget for original content production was $5 billion[8]), and second, that this video service was not a stand-alone package that people needed to purchase. Any Prime subscriber that would join Prime for the quick delivery of products or discounts (or some other reason) would get the video service tacked on, whether they wanted it or not—and might give it a try.
- *Hulu.* With over 20 million subscribers, Hulu's content focused on current and back season episodes of popular TV series. It also

contained a growing category of original content, spending an estimated $2.5 billion on original content in 2017.[9] At the time, Disney was increasing its ownership of Hulu through the purchase of Fox assets. Pricing-wise, Hulu uniquely offers a budget subscription that includes advertising for $8 per month, versus $12 for a regular subscription.

- *Disney.* For Disney, which already had a stake in Hulu and ESPN and owned many wildly popular brands from its own studios, including Marvel, Pixar, Star Wars, and National Geographic, entering the streaming market would be a logical next move. Its content was currently being offered through licensing deals with other streaming services like Netflix, but that content could be pulled and offered through Disney's own streaming service. Relative to the competition, Disney has a long history of developing original content, plus a large, existing portfolio of well-known brands and characters. Plus, it would have the ability to "cross-monetize" its various brands and assets between film, TV, music, and merchandizing.[10]

- *Apple.* Already offering Apple TV and having had experience building up a large subscriber base through Apple Music (with close to 60 million subscribers), Apple was in a likely position to be contemplating entering the online video streaming market. If it did, Apple would be in a cash flow position to spend heavily on the service, for example, on original content. With Apple TV and iPads as devices to stream content, and with iPhone sales dropping, offering a streaming service of its own could make a lot of sense to Apple CEO Tim Cook.

Step 4: Summarize insights from competitor analysis, including opportunities, gaps, and threats stemming from the analysis. The previous information offers some important opportunities and threats for Netflix going forward:

- *Threats.* Our analysis of competitors shows that the online streaming market is likely to get a lot more competitive for Netflix. Players up the value chain are planning to forward integrate, and content offered through Netflix on a licensing basis is likely to get pulled in the near future and offered through competing platforms. At the same time, some large, diversified competitors that have deep pockets and offer services that Netflix does not (like Amazon) are in, or are moving into, the space. Moreover, some of these players have a lot of experience developing content (Disney) or have an advantage on the end-user consumption side of things (Apple).

- *Opportunities.* There are also opportunities for Netflix. The in-flux of competition, paradoxically, may help Netflix by pushing even more reluctant members of the audience to cancel their cable subscription ("cut the cord") in favor of one or multiple streaming services. That is, people canceling their cable subscriptions frees up wallet space for multiple streaming services, which do not necessarily rival each other in the sense that one can easily have subscriptions to multiple streaming services. Plus, research from the British research agency Ampere supports the trend that people are spending less time watching "traditional" TV and more time using streaming platforms (an increase from 13% to 20% in a two-year period). Also important to bear in mind is that unlike companies like Disney, Netflix shareholders do not yet have high shareholder profit expectations, allowing Netflix to reinvest the lion's share of revenue toward developing ever better content. Finally, Netflix, at least at the time, being by far the biggest of the online streaming platforms in terms of users and content development budget, could reap scale advantages that so far have eluded its competitors.
- One important thought to include relates to the services' market positioning in terms of pricing. As for now, Netflix is at the top end of the market. Hulu charges $8 or $12 per month, the cheaper option including advertising. Amazon Video, at least in the United States, is included in a Prime membership. Apple and Disney pricing is for now unknown, but especially Disney is expected to come in at a price point below Netflix's.

Step 5: Derive strategic implications for the focal firm. So what can Netflix do to capitalize on the opportunities and mitigate the threats? Here are a few options:

- *Stay the course.* Despite the new competition coming in, Netflix was doing really well. Even with its astronomic original content development budget, Netflix was earning more revenue per subscriber than it was spending. Even if firms like Disney or Apple were able to capture a sizeable chunk of the market for streaming video, it is important to keep in mind that the market in and of itself was still growing. Also, people were expected to "multihome," that is, keep subscriptions to multiple streaming services.

- *Forward integrate.* At the time, there was significant vertical integration going on in the entertainment industry. Netflix had vertically integrated itself when it started producing original content in earnest itself. At the time, that was a novelty, but current and new competitors were mimicking this. Opportunities did exist, however, to forward integrate. Netflix relied on internet service providers and end-user devices (think smart TVs, phones, tablets, etc.) to generate the right conditions for content consumption. As this is an important part of the user experience, one could make the case that this is something Netflix would not want to rely on an outside partner for—particularly when this partner was fast becoming a competitor (think Apple).[11] In a sense, Netflix would be countering Apple's supposed competitive move by similarly moving yet in the opposite direction.

- *Reconsider positioning.* A third option that emerges from this analysis is that there may be opportunities to change Netflix's positioning through altering its pricing strategy. In late 2018, analysts expected most new competitors to come in at a subscription price below Netflix's price point. At first, when Netflix, being the first mover, was mainly competing with traditional TV subscriptions, it was much less expensive than cable, which was the natural reference point. With other firms offering similar services, that was fast becoming the new reference point. Should Netflix morph to being a differentiator or a cost leader? Its vision was to become "the best global entertainment distribution service," which would naturally seem to come with a price tag. However, an attempt to hike its price in 2016 resulted in lawsuits and cost Netflix an estimated half a million customers. Should it consider alternate pricing strategies, tagging on subscriptions to other services (like Amazon was doing), or drop its price to compete with less expensive alternatives? Here intimate knowledge of your customers is key. Research from consulting firm Magid reports that Netflix subscribers are less likely to cancel their service than customers of any other streaming platform. Would that carry forward if customers were able to combine competing services for the same price as one subscription to Netflix?

Step 6: Continue to monitor competitors over time. This essential step is often forgotten, but competitors, like the market they operate in, do not stand still. They too are constantly evaluating their offerings and strategic positioning relative to *their* main competitors. This leads to a dynamic cat-and-mouse game in which continuous monitoring and data collection on competitors are key, as is talking to customers to ensure you continue to offer superior value.

In conclusion, competitor analysis offers a useful lens to analyze Netflix's positioning relative to its competitors and offers some useful strategic directives. Particularly interesting for Netflix, given where its future competitors reside in the value chain, is the issue of forward and backward integration. For this very reason, we will return to Netflix in Chapter 14, where we will analyze Netflix through the lens of value chain analysis.

9
VRIO

Purpose and Objective

The purpose of VRIO analysis is to systematically identify resources and capabilities that may serve as a key source of competitive advantage. For a resource or capability to be the basis of a sustainable competitive advantage, it must be valuable (V), rare (R), and costly to imitate (I), and the firm must be organized (O) to capture the value from the resource or capability. These criteria allow managers and practitioners to assess any resource or capability to evaluate whether it may constitute a sustainable competitive advantage for a firm.

Underlying Theory

The VRIO framework has its roots in what is known as the resource-based view (RBV) of the firm. Tracing back to original work by Wernerfelt,[1] Barney,[2] and Rumelt,[3] the RBV essentially views firms as bundles of *resources*. Resources are defined as "those (tangible and intangible) assets which are tied semi-permanently to the firm."[4]

The RBV was born from the premise that a trend in scholarly research during the 1970s and 1980s (when research tended to focus heavily on an organization's environmental opportunities and threats) needed to be counterbalanced by an internal analysis of a firm's strengths and weaknesses. This premise is rooted in two fundamental assumptions, which differ from those implicitly underlying externally oriented models, such as those developed by Porter: (1) firms may be *heterogeneous* with respect to the strategic resources they control, and (2) resources are *sticky*, that is, not perfectly mobile across firms. Therefore, the RBV successfully redirected strategy scholars to resources as important antecedents for firm performance.[5] Arguably, the central logic of the RBV was proposed most clearly by Barney, who argued that possession of certain types of resources (those that are valuable, rare, difficult to imitate, and nonsubstitutable) can lead to sustained competitive advantage.[6]

Resources can take many different forms. One common classification[7] distinguishes between *financial resources, physical resources, human resources, technological resources, reputational resources*, and *organizational resources*. In essence, the RBV encapsulates the idea that a firm's competitive position is defined by the unique bundle of resources and relationships the firm possesses across these categories.

Core Idea

Resources and capabilities are assessed according to the criteria outlined in Table 9.1. If these criteria are met for a specific resource or capability, then that resource or capability may serve as a significant strength for the firm—something around which it can build a sustainable, competitive strategy.

Part of being effective as a manager or practitioner is identifying firm resources and capabilities that meet the VRIO criteria (or can meet the VRIO criteria) so that the foundation for a sustainable competitive advantage can be established.

Depiction

Figure 9.1 depicts the flow of the VRIO tool; it highlights the set of criteria that a manager can use to assess the internal resources and capabilities of a firm, and the order in which they should be assessed to see if they may contribute to sustained competitive advantage.[8]

Table 9.1 Assessing Resources and Capabilities for Sustainable Competitive Advantage

Criterion	Description	If Criterion Is Not Met
Valuable	A resource or capability is valuable if it helps a firm increase the perceived value of its products or services in the eyes of customers, either by adding attractive features or by lowering the cost of the product or service.	If a resource or capability is not valuable, then it does not provide any form of advantage.
Rare	A resource or capability is rare if only one or very few firms possess it. It must be something that other firms don't have.	If a resource or capability is not rare (i.e., it is common), then it will result in perfect competition, where no firm can maintain a competitive advantage.
costly to Imitate	A resource or capability is costly to imitate if firms that do not possess it are unable to develop or buy it at a reasonable price. Sometimes laws (e.g., patent or trademark laws, property laws) make a resource difficult or costly to imitate. Other times less obvious reasons make a resource or capability difficult to imitate, such as: • *Historical conditions and path dependence.* Resources that are developed over a long period of time and dependent on a progressive series of decisions and actions are usually costly to imitate. • *Causal ambiguity.* The cause and effect of phenomena giving rise to competitive advantage are not clear. • *Social complexity.* Different social and business systems interact with one another in complex ways, making them difficult and costly to replicate or imitate.	If a resource or capability is not costly to imitate, then other firms are likely to develop or buy it, and when they do, competitive advantage may be eroded.

Continued

Table 9.1 Continued

Criterion	Description	If Criterion Is Not Met
Organized to capture value	A firm is organized to capture value from a resource or capability if it has an organizational structure and coordinating mechanisms in place that allow them to leverage that resource or capability into the marketplace in an efficient and effective way.	If a firm is not organized to capture value from a resource or capability, then even though it has something that is valuable, rare, and costly to imitate, it may fail to generate profits because it cannot deliver and capture value in a reasonable and sustainable way.

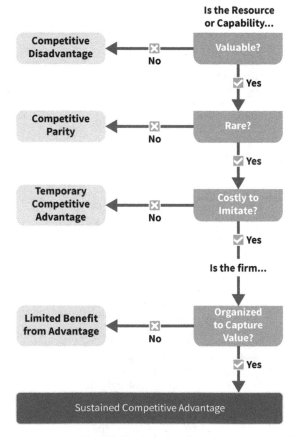

Figure 9.1. VRIO tool to assess a firm's internal resources and capabilities.

Process

1. Identify valuable resources or capabilities. The following questions may help to identify valuable resources and capabilities:
   - Which activities lower the cost of production without decreasing perceived customer value?
   - Which activities increase product or service differentiation and perceived customer value?
   - Has your company won an award or been recognized as the best in class (e.g., most innovative, best employer, highest customer retention, best exporter)?
   - Do you have access to scarce raw materials or hard-to-access distribution channels?
   - Do you have a special relationship with your suppliers, such as a tightly integrated order and distribution system powered by unique software?
   - Do you have employees with unique skills and capabilities?
   - Do you have brand reputation for quality, innovation, and/or customer service?
   - Do you perform any tasks better than your competitors do?
   - Does your company have any other strengths compared to rivals?
2. Assess whether valuable resources or capabilities are rare. The following questions may help to assess whether valuable resources and capabilities are also rare:
   - How many other companies own a resource or deliver this capability in the same way in your industry?
   - Can the resource or capability be acquired in the market by rivals?
3. Assess whether valuable and rare resources or capabilities are costly to imitate. The following questions may help to assess whether valuable and rare resources and capabilities are also costly to imitate:
   - Can other companies easily duplicate the resource or capability?
   - Can competitors easily develop a substitute resource?

- Do patents or other laws protect it?
- Is a resource or capability socially complex?
- Is it hard to identify the particular processes, tasks, or other factors that form the resource?

4. Assess whether the focal firm is organized to exploit these resources or capabilities. The following questions might be helpful to assess whether a firm is organized to capture value from a resource or capability:
   - Does the company have an effective strategic management process in place?
   - Are there effective motivation and reward systems in place?
   - Is the organizational structure designed to use a resource?
   - Are there effective management and control systems?

5. Use a resource or capability that has been identified as valuable, rare, or costly to imitate, and for which a firm is (or can be) organized to capture value as the cornerstone or focal point for developing a broader strategy. In so doing seek to exploit and protect the resource or capability that is valuable, rare, and costly to imitate.

Insight or Value Created

VRIO provides a means for managers and practitioners to focus on a firm's most valuable elements when developing a strategy. It allows them to uncover and exploit true sources of competitive advantage to develop distinctiveness in a marketplace.

Barney and Hesterley argue that VRIO is an integrative framework that connects ideas together. They are of the view that VRIO allows managers and practitioners "to discuss the formulation and implementation of strategy simultaneously."[9]

Risks and Limitations

VRIO is sometimes criticized for creating an inward-looking perspective of strategy. It may prompt managers and practitioners to focus within firm boundaries to identify strategic options and thereby miss options that come about as changes occur outside the firm.

VRIO is also sometimes criticized for creating a backward-looking, or static, perspective of strategy. It tends to focus on what a firm has and where it has been rather than on where it is going. It fails to account for the dynamic environment in which current firms operate and hence may miss opportunities and threats that emerge from changes in the firm's environment. For this reason, some practitioners argue that it is important to do a VRIO analysis in conjunction with a macro-environmental (STEEP) analysis. Another response to this criticism is the development of a dynamic capabilities perspective of strategy. A dynamic capability is the capability of an organization to purposefully adapt an organization's resource base. The concept has been defined as "the firm's ability to integrate, build, and reconfigure internal and external competencies to address rapidly changing environments."[10]

Researchers have discovered that managers using a VRIO framework to evaluate and formulate a strategy may also overlook firm weaknesses and threats as a result of only looking for what is valuable, rare, and costly to imitate within a firm.[11]

Case Illustration: Harley-Davidson

Context

To illustrate VRIO analysis, we return to a case we discussed before in Chapter 7 on five-forces analysis, that of Harley-Davidson. Recall that from mid-2015 onward, the U.S.-based motorcycle manufacturer started facing some significant challenges and took a big hit in profitability. On the basis of our five-forces analysis, we concluded that Harley's traditional industry position was becoming less attractive. However, few would formulate a new strategy solely based on an analysis of the attractiveness of the industry segment. Instead, one would also want to look internally at the resources Harley-Davidson wields, and which of those are VRIO.

Assessing Harley-Davidson's Resource Mix

To ascertain which of Harley's resources were valuable, rare, and hard to imitate, and which Harley was organized around to capture value from, we need to go through the following steps:

Step 1: Identify valuable resources or capabilities. Harley commanded quite a long list of valuable resources and capabilities. While the following list is certainly not exhaustive, these resources and capabilities are definitely worth mentioning as meeting the criterion of being valuable in the 2015–2018 period on which we focus our analysis:

- Manufacturing
- Brand image
- Domestic market share
- Distribution, dealer network
- Product design
- Customer relationship
- Research and development (R&D)
- Supplier network
- Product quality
- Marketing

Now, we hold each of these resources and capabilities to the criteria of rarity, imitability, and whether Harley is organized to really capture value from it.

Step 2: Assess whether valuable resources or capabilities are rare. Now let us apply the questions and criteria of rarity to the previous list:

- *Manufacturing.* Harley's motorcycle manufacturing expertise, particularly for heavyweight bikes, was certainly valuable, but was it also rare? Clearly, this is not clear-cut black and white, but rather a matter of interpretation. Analysts seem to agree, however, that similar manufacturing capabilities were held by major competitors like BMW, Ducati, Honda, Kawasaki, Suzuki, and Yamaha.

- *Brand image.* The only American motorcycle brand has never gone out of business,[12] Harley-Davidson was one of the most iconic, powerful, and recognizable brands in America and the world, which is very, very rare and next to impossible to replicate.
- *Domestic market share.* Harley-Davidson has traditionally commanded a huge market share, particularly domestically (currently at just over 50% in key segments), which hardly any competitor had in respective markets.
- *Distribution, dealer network.* Harley commands a vast dealer network of currently (2018) over 1500 dealerships (1435 in 2015), of which roughly 700 are in the United States, 400 in Europe, and 300 in Asia. Again, this is quite rare.
- *Product design.* Harleys had a typical look and feel that appealed to a broad generation of riders. Being able to generate this typical look and feel is valuable and rare.
- *Customer relationship.* Harley has had a special relationship with its key traditional customers, as evidenced in the Harley lifestyle. As one Harley owner commented, "You don't get a tattoo of Honda."[13]
- *R&D.* Even through the recessions (which Harley survived), R&D has always been a key focus of Harley-Davidson's, as evidenced in its R&D expenditure and attention to typical elements of the Harley experience, including having a jury rate the sound of each new model.[14] We would assess this as being both valuable and rare.
- *Supplier network.* Harley held long-term relationships with a relatively tight set of suppliers, which is certainly valuable, but among the major competitors, this is not exceedingly rare in terms of quality or cost leadership.
- *Product quality.* Harley's product quality is valuable, and again, while not clear-cut black and white, experts seemed to agree that Harley's quality is not exceedingly rare compared to the

main competitors (BMW, Ducati, Honda, Kawasaki, Suzuki, and Yamaha).

- *Marketing.* Besides traditional marketing channels, Harley-Davidson's marketing efforts have long emphasized events like group rides and rallies. This is valuable, but also rare, and related to the lifestyle that is associated with Harley-Davidson.

Step 3: Assess whether valuable and rare resources or capabilities are costly to imitate. Now we assess the remaining set of resources and capabilities (those found to be valuable and rare) through the I of imitation, using the questions presented earlier in this chapter:

- *Brand image.* Being one of the most iconic, powerful, and recognizable brands in America and the world is next to impossible to replicate, hence also meeting the criteria of being hard to imitate.
- *Domestic market share.* Replicating Harley's huge market share, particularly in its domestic market, is very hard to do, and hence also meets the criterion of being hard to imitate.
- *Distribution, dealer network.* Harley's vast dealer network was valuable and quite rare, and very hard to imitate by competitors.
- *Product design.* Harley's typical look and feel is valuable and rare but has been imitated and later surpassed by competitors who were more in tune with the rise of a new generation of riders and designed sleeker, lighter, less "chrome-looking" bikes. Hence, we would rate product design for Harley as valuable and rare but not exceedingly hard to imitate by its competitors.
- *Customer relationship.* The special relationship Harley had with its customers is very hard to imitate as it requires human emotion and being able to strike the right tone with customers.
- *R&D.* R&D for Harley was valuable, rare, and hard to imitate as in addition to financial resources R&D requires specialized knowledge and skills.
- *Marketing.* The event-based side of Harley-Davidson's marketing was hard to replicate, as it requires a special kind of bond with customers to show up at rides and rallies in large numbers.

Step 4: Assess whether the focal firm is organized to exploit these resources or capabilities. Finally, we see which of the remaining resources and capabilities on the list are also meeting the criterion of currently being exploited by the firm to drive revenue.

- *Brand image.* Harley-Davidson was still trying to effectively exploit its brand image, even though it would soon need to be updated. Randy McBee, author of the motorcycle history book *Born to Be Wild*, was quoted as saying: "That whole biker-with-his-T-shirt-sleeves-cut-off image has finally caught up with them,"[15] and a new generation was hesitant to embrace it. One might therefore state that Harley-Davidson was doing a suboptimal job of exploiting its stellar brand awareness and reputation in the United States. Overseas, however, that was not necessarily the case, and that was where the growth was coming from.
- *Domestic market share.* While domestic market share was strong, the motorcycle market in the United States was not. In fact, growth was mainly coming from overseas markets and different types of segments. Therefore, Harley was not really exploiting its domestic market share to the full extent.
- *Distribution, dealer network.* Harley-Davidson's vast and hard to imitate dealer network provided a potential source of competitive advantage, but was felt to not be capitalized to the full extent. It was recognized that selling an increasingly diverse product to an increasingly diverse customer base would require the dealership network to be considerably strengthened. Harley-Davidson's network particularly lacked an urban presence, exactly where new customer segments might be reached. Digital capabilities to reach customers directly through ecommerce were also felt to be under-exploited.
- *Customer relationship.* Harley was still exploiting its relationship to existing customers, but at the same time, those typical customers were aging and Harley did not manage to build a similar relationship with new customers yet.
- *R&D.* At the time, Harley was experimenting with a number of quite different products, but those had not yet taken off. Still, an impressive lineup of new models more aligned with a new generation of riders was being developed.

- *Marketing.* Harley's marketing machine was still firing on all cylinders, trying to keep selling the Harley lifestyle. At the same time, marketing was still directed by and large at the traditional customer base. Some were even worried that outreach to a different type of customer might alienate Harley's existing customer base. For this reason, Harley was only partially exploiting this resource.

The VRIO analysis is summarized in Table 9.2.

Step 5: Use a resource or capability that has been identified as valuable, rare, and costly to imitate, and for which a firm is (or can be) organized to capture value as the cornerstone or focal point for developing a broader strategy. From this analysis, the resources and capabilities that Harley-Davidson controlled that were valuable, rare, and costly to imitate, and for which the firm is *or could be* organized to exploit, are the following:

- Brand image
- Domestic market share
- Distribution and dealer network

Table 9.2 Summary of the VRIO Analysis for Harley-Davidson

Resource or Capability	Valuable	Rare	Costly to Imitate	Exploited
Manufacturing	X			
Brand image	X	X	X	
Domestic market share	X	X	X	
Distribution, dealer network	X	X	X	
Product design	X	X		
Customer relationship	X	X	X	
R&D	X	X	X	X
Supplier network	X			
Product quality	X			
Marketing	X	X	X	

- Customer relationship
- R&D
- Marketing

From these, we felt that only one was really being exploited at the time. The rest formed formidable opportunities for a strategic reassessment.

Interestingly, Harley's new strategy, which at the time was soon to be launched, mirrored the previous analysis of resources and capabilities, focused on building and reinforcing Harley-Davidson's domestic market share by "building 2 million new riders in the U.S."; maintaining its premium brand and taking it internationally to grow its international sales; maintaining good customer relationships by always "serving the customer" and "meeting customers where they are"; capitalizing on R&D by launching "100 New High Impact Harley-Davidson Motorcycles," including small displacement motorcycles and electric motorcycles; focusing on stronger dealers and broader access; and boosting marketing by offering an "integrated retail experience" and "new retail formats."

10

Financial Performance Analysis

Purpose and Objective

The purpose of analyzing a firm's financial performance is two-fold. Not only does it illuminate the economic health of an organization relative to its selected peer group, but also it aids in assessing the efficacy of managerial decisions and associate adverse consequences with root causes. Analyzing a company's financial performance can be an important first step in understanding the outcomes of implemented strategies. Financial performance analysis therefore provides not only a basis for justifying existing strategies but also insights that inform alterations to the current course of action.

When used to evaluate and determine strategy, financial performance analysis prompts managers to look for causation between their decisions and economic success. It encourages managers and practitioners to measure impact using tangible metrics.

Underlying Theory

Financial statements represent the formal record of the results from economic activity and the position of a business.

The *balance sheet* represents the assets owned by a company, the liabilities owed to others, and the investments made by its owners. It serves as a snapshot of a company's business at a given point in time and illustrates how the sum of a company's liabilities and owner's equity balances with its assets.

The *income statement* represents a summary of the revenues generated and the expenses incurred by an entity for a period of time. It highlights the net income or net loss incurred by a company as a result of its normal operating activities.

Financial performance analysis seeks to identify the strengths and weaknesses of a firm by drawing clear relationships between information on the balance sheet and that contained in the income statement. According to Metcalf and Titard,[1] "it is a process of evaluating the relationship parts of [the] financial statement for better understanding of a firm's position and performance."

There are numerous methods used to analyze financial statements, including comparative financial statement analysis, common size balance sheets, statement of changes in working capital, trend analysis, and funds analysis. However, the most common approach to analyzing financial statements in an integrative fashion is the use of financial ratios, which combine elements from both the balance sheet and income statement.

Core Idea

The core idea behind financial performance analysis is to use the firm's own performance to identify opportunities to improve the execution of its corporate or business unit strategy. The company's strategy dictates a series of tactics, the outcomes of which are reflected in the company's financial performance. As a result, the core idea is to use the results from the implementation of these tactics to evaluate the efficacy of the strategy and make adjustments.

The summative financial metric for publicly traded companies is total return to shareholders (TRS), which measures the cumulative return to shareholders over a given period of time. Commonly referred to as "value created," TRS is a function of discounted cash flow, derived through spread and growth. Value can be created when the difference between return on invested capital (ROIC) and the company's weighted average cost of capital (WACC) is increased, or magnified when the return is increased through growth in cash flow. The calculation for TRS is as follows:

((Ending Stock Price + Accumulated Dividends) / Beginning Stock Price) – 1

Beyond this summative metric, there are a number of more specific financial ratios that can be calculated to provide even greater insight on firm performance. These ratios are commonly organized around the following:

- Liquidity—Measures of the ability of a company to pay its debts when they fall due. Liquidity is the ability to pay short-term obligations and is a signal to the market of a firm's short-term solvency.
- Operating activities—Measures the general flow of cash to fund the manufacturing and selling of goods and services. Ratios related to operating activities are an indication of the efficiency of operations.
- Leverage—Measures the company's use of debt and/or credit to purchase physical assets or fund operating activities. Leverage ratios are a signal of a firm's long-term solvency.
- Profitability—Measures the extent to which a company manages the spread between the cost of goods sold and the prices charged for its goods and services.

For a complete list of the key financial ratios for each, please refer to the graphical depiction in Figure 10.1.

Depiction

Figure 10.1 highlights all the key ratios that can be assessed in a financial performance analysis, and it shows how these different ratios fit together into a coherent whole.[2]

	Ratio	Calculation	Location	Definition
LIQUIDITY	CURRENT	Total Current Assets / Total Current Liabilities	Balance Sheet	Measures solvency and the ability for current assets to be used to meet current liabilities
	QUICK	Cash + Marketable Securities + Accounts Receivable - Inventories / Current Liabilities	Balance Sheet	Measures how quickly a company can turn its current assets into cash
ACTIVITY	AVERAGE COLLECTION PERIOD	Average Accounts Receivable / (Total Sales / Days in Period)	Balance Sheet Income Statement	Measures the average number of days it takes to collect an account receivable
	INVENTORY TURNOVER	Cost of Goods Sold / Inventory	Income Statement Balance Sheet	Measures how quickly inventory is sold
	AVERAGE PAYMENT PERIOD	Average Accounts Payable / (Total Credit Purchases / Days in Period)	Balance Sheet Income Statement	Measures the average number of days it takes a business to pay its vendors
	FIXED ASSET TURNOVER	Sales / Net Fixed Assets	Income Statement Balance Sheet	Measures the efficiency of fixed assets
	TOTAL ASSET TURNOVER	Sales / Total Assets	Income Statement Balance Sheet	Overall measure of asset management efficiency
LEVERAGE	DEBT TO ASSETS	Total Debt / Total Assets	Balance Sheet	Measures the percentage of assets financed by creditors
	DEBT TO EQUITY	Total Debt / Total Shareholder's Equity	Balance Sheet	Measures the funds provided by creditors versus funds provided by owners
	INTEREST COVERAGE	Earnings Before Interest and Taxes (EBIT) / Interest Expense	Income Statement	Measures how much of a company's interest obligations are covered by earnings
	FIXED CHARGE COVERAGE	EBIT + Lease Payments / ((Interest + Lease Payments + Principal / (1 - Taxes))	Income Statement	Measures how much of a company's total obligations are covered by earnings
PROFITABILITY	GROSS MARGIN	Gross Profit / Total Sales	Income Statement	Measures the remaining sales dollars after cost of goods sold have been deducted
	NET MARGIN	Earnings After Tax (EAT) / Total Sales	Income Statement	Measures the remaining sales dollars after all of the company's expenses have been deducted
	RETURN ON ASSETS	EBIT / Total Assets	Income Statement Balance Sheet	Measures the return to both shareholders and creditors on total assets
	RETURN ON EQUITY	EAT / Total Shareholder's Equity	Income Statement Balance Sheet	Measures the return to shareholders
	EARNINGS PER SHARE	EAT / Average Number of Total Common Shares Outstanding	Income Statement Balance Sheet	Measures the portion of a company's profit allocated to each share of common stock
	PRICE TO EARNINGS	Current Share Price / Earnings Per Share	Income Statement	Measures stock market confidence that earnings will lead to cash inflows in the future

Figure 10.1. Financial analysis tool to assess a firm's financial position and performance.

Process

1. Select peer companies for comparison purposes using either Standard Industrial Classification (SIC) or North American Industry Classification Systems (NAICS) codes.
2. Calculate TRS for both the target company and industry peers. (Skip this step if target company is not publicly traded.)
3. Analyze returns and look for anomalies. Discrepancies may exist within the target company over a period of time, between the target company and peers, or among the chosen peer group. (Skip this step if target company is not publicly traded.)
4. Calculate key financial ratios related to firm liquidity, operating activity, debt utilization (leverage), and profitability.
5. Analyze returns and look for anomalies. Discrepancies may exist within the target company over a period of time, between the target company and peers, or among the chosen peer group.
6. For specific discrepancies, perform a root-cause analysis to determine the source of the discrepancy and offer mitigating strategies.

Insight or Value Created

A common critique of strategic analysis is the perceived lack of follow-through between diagnose and decide, and deliver. Financial performance analysis can be used as the bridge between strategic decisions and the measurement of strategic delivery. This is done by associating strategic choices made by the firm with the economic outcomes of these decisions as reflected in key financial ratios.

Financial performance analysis also provides a holistic way to interpret a company's financial health. While the income statement evolves and has a tendency to change from one account period to the next, the balance sheet tends to be more stable. Connecting the integrated analysis by calculating key financial ratios helps deliver more robust insights into the company's performance than either can deliver separately.

Risks and Limitations

There are two predominant limitations of financial performance analysis. First, the financial reporting data that forms the basis of this analysis reflects historical information on company performance. While this may be helpful in assessing the efficacy of decisions made in the past, it is limited in terms of its utility in predicting the probability of success for future actions. As market conditions are in a constant state of change, factors that led to economic gain in the past may no longer be an accurate predictor of similar gains in the future.

Second, also inherent to the process of financial performance analysis is the limitations of using industry peers to assess firm health. The consequence of benchmarking against industry peers is that a company may become overly focused on measures of competitive parity, rather than seeking true innovations and sources of sustainable competitive advantage.

Case Illustration: Coca-Cola and PepsiCo

Context

It has been over a century since Coca-Cola and Pepsi began competing directly for market share in the global beverage market. Operating in a healthy duopoly, both companies have benefited greatly from the ability of each to command dominating positions that have essentially prevented other upstarts from becoming significant players on the global stage.

Americans consumed fifty-three gallons of carbonated soft drinks annually in 2000. Since then, consumption has steadily dropped. As illustrated in Figure 10.2, consumption declined to fewer than forty gallons by the end of 2017.

Although the most direct battles between these two companies through the years were fought in the United States over its $74 billion carbonated soft drink market, the leadership of both companies recognize the benefits of the implied coopetition that has emerged.

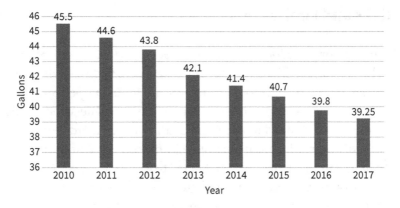

Figure 10.2. The per capita consumption of carbonated drinks in the United States over time.

As an example, in 2013, when PepsiCo CEO Indra Nooyi was asked on India's CBNC-TV 18 about her company's plans to invest in its Indian operations, she responded by saying, "I think we all know that the beverage industry has two great companies. Two great companies that collectively are going to invest $10.5 billion in India. That's the sort of discussion we should be having—not C versus P, which is irrelevant."[3]

Analyzing Financial Performance to Illuminate Competitive Positioning

Faced with diminishing domestic sales of carbonated soft drinks, both Coke and Pepsi face strategic questions about how best to ensure sustainable growth and profitability. These questions include not only whether or not they can boost carbonated soft drink sales but also how they can compete in a growing noncarbonated category that demands very different approaches.

To generate strategic solutions to address their growth concerns, it would benefit both Pepsi and Coca-Cola to perform a financial performance analysis. To illustrate the process of conducting the analysis, let us go through the steps described earlier in the chapter and apply them to this intense competition.

Step 1: Select peer companies for basis of comparison. In this context, we are seeking a head-to-head comparison between two firms. However, in most situations, the list of peer companies that form the basis of comparison are both numerous and not always known in advance. A quick scan of the SIC codes reveals that both PepsiCo and Coca-Cola operate primarily in SIC Code 5149—Groceries and Related Products. Other beverage companies that are also listed under this code include Dr. Pepper Snapple Group Inc., Polar Beverages, and Monster Beverage Corp., all of which may be appropriate to include based on the intent of the analysis.

Step 2: Calculate total return to shareholders. As stated earlier in the chapter, the calculation for TRS is as follows:

((Ending Stock Price + Accumulated Dividends) / Beginning Stock Price) – 1

Using this formula, we calculate TRS for both companies:

PepsiCo: $((110.48 + 3.5875) / 118.06) - 1 = -3\%$

Coke: $((177.38 + 1.56) / 211.28) - 1 = -15\%$

Step 3: Analyze returns. The previous TRS calculation tells us how much a dollar invested in either of these companies increased or decreased in value over the given year. For 2018, we see the TRS of both PepsiCo and Coca-Cola to be indicative of sluggish global economic trends for the year. PepsiCo may have been the better value for the year, but it is clear that both companies are facing significant headwinds in returning shareholder value, which aligns well with the challenges described earlier with growing the core carbonated soft drink business.

Step 4: Calculate key financial ratios. Given the challenges with creating shareholder value that both companies faced in 2018, we next turn our attention to providing greater clarity on the financial health of each company by completing the calculation of key financial ratios. The completed analysis presented in Figure 10.3 is an integrative view of the financial performance of both companies. It may also be informative to compare this analysis to

Key Financial Ratios - Coca Cola (KO) vs Pepsi (PEP) Fiscal Year 2018

	Ratio	Calculation*	Coca-Cola		Pepsi	
Liquidity	Current	$\frac{\text{Total Current Assets}}{\text{Total Current Liabilities}}$ $\frac{30.634}{29.223}$		1.05	$\frac{21.839}{22.138}$	0.99
	Quick	$\frac{\text{Cash + Marketable Securities + Accounts Receivable - Inventories}}{\text{Current Liabilities}}$ $\frac{17.335}{29.223}$		0.59	$\frac{13.007}{22.138}$	0.59
Activity	Average Collection Period	$\frac{\text{Average Accounts Receivable}}{\text{(Total Sales / Days in Period)}}$ $\frac{3.381}{0.08}$		42	$\frac{7.083}{0.17}$	42
	Inventory Turnover	$\frac{\text{Cost of Goods Sold}}{\text{Inventory}}$ $\frac{11.77}{2.766}$		4.26	$\frac{29.381}{3.128}$	9.39
	Average Payment Period	$\frac{\text{Average Accounts Payable}}{\text{(Total Credit Purchases / Days in Period)}}$ $\frac{8.84}{0.115}$		77	$\frac{16.564}{0.184}$	90
	Fixed Asset Turnover	$\frac{\text{Sales}}{\text{Net Fixed Assets}}$ $\frac{31.856}{8.232}$		3.87	$\frac{64.661}{17.589}$	3.68
	Total Asset Turnover	$\frac{\text{Sales}}{\text{Total Assets}}$ $\frac{31.856}{83.216}$		0.38	$\frac{64.661}{77.648}$	0.83
leverage	Debt to Assets	$\frac{\text{Total Debt}}{\text{Total Assets}}$ $\frac{43.555}{83.216}$		0.52	$\frac{63.046}{77.648}$	0.81
	Debt to Equity	$\frac{\text{Total Debt}}{\text{Total Shareholder's Equity}}$ $\frac{43.555}{16.981}$		2.56	$\frac{63.046}{14.518}$	4.34
	Interest Coverage	$\frac{\text{Earnings Before Interest and Taxes (EBIT)}}{\text{Interest Expense}}$ $\frac{9.269}{0.919}$		10.09	$\frac{10.110}{1.525}$	6.63
Profitability	Gross Margin	$\frac{\text{Gross Profit}}{\text{Total Sales}}$ $\frac{20.086}{31.856}$		63%	$\frac{35.280}{64.661}$	55%
	Net Margin	$\frac{\text{Earnings After Tax (EAT)}}{\text{Total Sales}}$ $\frac{6.434}{31.856}$		20%	$\frac{12.513}{64.661}$	19%
	Return on Assets	$\frac{\text{EBIT}}{\text{Total Assets}}$ $\frac{9.269}{83.216}$		11%	$\frac{10.110}{77.648}$	13%
	Return on Equity	$\frac{\text{Net Income}}{\text{Total Shareholder's Equity}}$ $\frac{6.434}{16.981}$		38%	$\frac{12.513}{14.518}$	86%
	Earnings Per Share	$\frac{\text{Net Income}}{\text{Average Number of Total Common Shares Outstanding}}$ $\frac{6.434}{4.259}$		1.51	$\frac{12.513}{1.415}$	8.84
	Price to Earnings	$\frac{\text{Current Share Price}}{\text{Earnings Per Share}}$ $\frac{46.94}{1.51}$		31.09	$\frac{108.79}{8.78}$	12.39

* (in billions)

Figure 10.3. Analysis of the financial position and performance of Coca-Cola and Pepsi.

previous years to establish trends in financial performance that may not be discovered by looking at just a single year of actual performance.

Step 5: Analyze ratios. Once we have completed the calculations, we can use the ratio analysis to identify sources of both advantage and disadvantage based on the favorability of each position based on actual market performance. In this instance, a few insights can be generated from such a comparison:

1. For 2018, PepsiCo had a more favorable return on equity, increasing investor confidence in PepsiCo's market capitalization and ability to create value for shareholders.
2. Enjoying the benefits of a less diverse portfolio of businesses, Coca-Cola is more efficient than PepsiCo in matching production with market demand as exhibited by its significantly shorter inventory turnover times.
3. Coca-Cola has a distinct advantage in gross profit compared to Pepsi but has opportunities to improve its operational efficiency to maintain this advantage after the cost of operations is taken into effect.

Step 6: Offer mitigating strategies based on identified discrepancies. Using insights generated from this financial performance analysis, several opportunities are provided here for each company to explore further through more robust strategic hypothesis testing.

PepsiCo.
- Given its strong return on equity compared to Coca-Cola, Pepsi will have little trouble convincing equity markets of its ability to generate value from additional requests for capital. Stock issuance for investment opportunities are likely to be viewed favorably, and Pepsi can leverage this to fund expansion efforts in the noncarbonated category.
- Although Pepsi's product portfolio is much more diverse than Coca-Cola's, Pepsi's inventory turnover suggests that opportunities to either improve demand planning or identify new distribution channels for its products may lead to value creation for the company.

Coca-Cola
- Strategic initiatives that target reducing the cost to serve and leverage the scale of Coke's vast operations in bottling and distribution represent significant opportunities.

- Coca-Cola has invested close to $5 billion more in fixed assets like plants, property, and equipment than Pepsi, yet it trails Pepsi in revenue generated from those assets almost two to one. Opportunities to use existing physical assets more efficiently could unlock additional sales potential and increase top-line growth.

11

SWOT

Purpose and Objective

A SWOT analysis is a simple way to examine a firm's current situation by accounting for a firm's strengths, weaknesses, opportunities, and threats. It provides a means to account for internal and external factors plus positive and negative factors confronting a firm, thereby providing a balanced perspective of strategic issues. The SWOT analysis was developed as a means to establish the strategic fit between a company's internal environment (its resources and capabilities) and its external environment. A SWOT analysis provides a basis to identify how a firm might use its strengths to exploit opportunities and defend its strengths while overcoming weaknesses to defend against threats.

Underlying Theory

Despite its wide prevalence, the origin of the term *SWOT* is unknown. Helms and Nixon,[1] in their review of SWOT analysis use, trace SWOT analysis back to a study by Learned and colleagues;[2] however, online wikis credit SWOT's origination with Stanford University professor Albert Humphrey, who led a research project in the 1960s and 1970s based on the United States' Fortune 500 companies, but no academic references to support this claim can be found.

Although there has been confusion regarding who should take credit for coining the term *SWOT*, the SWOT framework is one of the most well-known and prevalent strategy frameworks. This popularity is interesting in and of itself, because SWOT analysis is, in the eyes of the scholarly community, remarkably undertheorized. In the words of Grant,[3] the research community has tended to view SWOT as "a theoretic classificatory system" and has criticized the framework for lacking *theoretical support* to validate the model,[4] for being *vague and overly simplistic*,[5] and for not providing a *clear strategic direction*.[6]

Various researchers have responded to these criticisms by trying to rework and extend traditional SWOT analysis with elements from the resource-based view, five-forces analysis, and a host of other more complex yet conceptually more robust tools. None of these, however, seem to have had the appeal to the business world that the original SWOT idea has had. That is, despite extensive criticism from management theorists, all around the world hordes of real-world strategists resort to SWOT analysis as an initial tool to start a strategy process on a daily basis.

Core Idea

The core idea behind doing a SWOT analysis is to systematically identify a firm's strengths, weaknesses, opportunities, and threats. Strengths and weaknesses tend to focus on internal issues, related to the firm's past and current position. Opportunities and threats focus on the future external environment in which a firm is likely to operate. The analysis of opportunities and threats may be significantly informed by a macro-environmental (STEEP) analysis (see Chapter 6). The analysis of strengths may be significantly informed by a VRIO analysis (see Chapter 9). The elements of a SWOT analysis are summarized in Table 11.1.

Depiction

The concept of a SWOT analysis is depicted in Figure 11.1. This figure shows how SWOT brings together internal and external

Table 11.1 Elements of a SWOT Analysis

Element	Description
Strengths	Factors that make a firm more competitive than its rivals; areas in which a firm has superior resources or capabilities compared to competition. Strengths tend to focus on internal factors that are currently under firm's control.
Weaknesses	Limitations, faults, or defects within a firm that prevent it from achieving its strategic objectives. They cause a firm to underperform in serving customers relative to competitors. Weaknesses tend to focus on current, internal factors that impede a firm's performance.
Opportunities	Any favorable current or prospective situation in the external environment. A trend, force, or change in the external environment that may place the firm in a more favorable position may underlie an opportunity. Opportunities can allow firms to convert weaknesses into strengths or leverage strengths to increase advantages.
Threats	Unfavorable trends, forces, and changes in the external environment that have the potential to erode a firm's ability to compete. Threats can turn strengths into weaknesses.

perspectives, in both a positive and negative light, and leverages insights from other tools such as VRIO and STEEP.

Figure 11.2 shows how SWOT elements can be combined to generate interesting and relevant strategic options for a firm. In doing this, SWOT shifts from a backward-looking to forward-looking tool.

Process

1. List and evaluate SWOT elements.
2. Analyze and rank factors within each category of strengths, weaknesses, opportunities, and threats.
3. Combine categories to identify actions and options that link internal and external factors.
   a. Combine strengths and opportunities to identify how a firm might leverage strengths to seize opportunities or utilize opportunities to reinforce strengths.

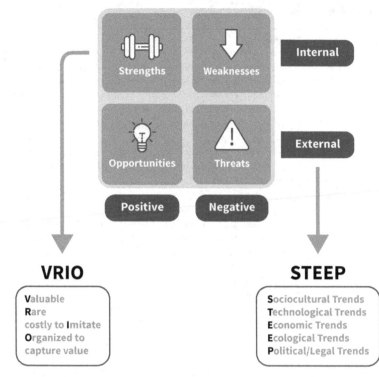

Figure 11.1. SWOT analysis to assess internal and external factors plus positive and negative factors affecting a firm.

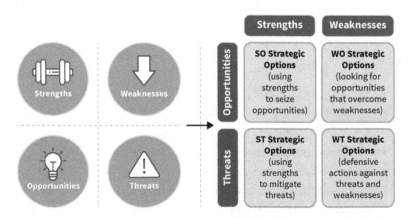

Figure 11.2. Combining SWOT factors to generate strategic options for a firm.

b. Combine weaknesses and opportunities to identify how a firm might use opportunities to overcome weaknesses.

c. Combine strengths and threats to identify how a firm might leverage strengths to mitigate threats.

d. Combine weaknesses and threats to identify how a firm defends against a combination of weaknesses and threats.

4. Look at all actions and options and use them to inform overall strategic decisions.

Insight or Value Created

A SWOT analysis is useful for organizing large amounts of disparate data about a firm. It is a simple and understandable framework that connects internal and external data.

SWOT allows managers and practitioners to prioritize issues that have the greatest impact on a firm and its competitiveness.

The simplicity of SWOT means that people of all levels and skills can participate in and understand the analysis. This can serve as an excellent base to guide and prompt further strategic discussions and analysis.

Risks and Limitations

SWOT is sometimes criticized for being overly simple and hence masking complexity. People may categorize things without carefully considering the root causes or issues.

Interpretation of information generated by a SWOT analysis is likely to vary between different managers and practitioners. Different interpretations may prompt different strategic conclusions, which can be difficult to reconcile.

SWOT was developed at a time when industries where less dynamic; therefore, SWOT is sometimes criticized for being static and only providing a snapshot of a situation, as compared to a dynamic perspective that changes over time.

SWOT analysis mostly reflects and highlights issues confronting a firm, but such an analysis does not really identify key actions to be taking. Therefore, it is criticized for not providing enough guidance about what needs to be done within a firm.

Sometimes people within a firm find it difficult to conduct a SWOT analysis because they are too close to what is going on in that firm. For this reason, it can be useful to get the input of objective outsiders to provide perspective when conducting a SWOT analysis.

Case Illustration: The Chocolate Moose

Context

Located in Bloomington, Indiana, the Chocolate Moose is an independently owned and operated ice cream shop that began in 1933. The shop is located conveniently in downtown Bloomington, a college town of approximately 50,000 residents. It specializes in homemade soft-serve ice cream and yogurt. The unassuming walk-up ice cream stand is a cultural landmark for many Bloomingtonians, holding a deep sentimental attachment for long-time residents.

The Chocolate Moose sells its products at a small, leased property, as well as in local grocery stores and restaurants. Committed regulars have kept the Chocolate Moose thriving for years. Even though it has enjoyed over eighty years of success, its business is subject to seasonal variation. Figure 11.3 depicts the Chocolate Moose's revenue by month for the years 2012–2015.

In the spring of 2015, two significant external events became a cause of concern. First, the Chocolate Moose's landlord informed the owners that he intended to sell the parcel of land their store and production facility resided on. Second, and equally as alarming, the City of Bloomington had just recently announced plans to modernize the downtown area, including widening and repaving the street on which the store stood. For most of the next three years, the only way to access the parking lot would be on foot. Combined, these two events would inevitably lead to a decline in business, and the owners

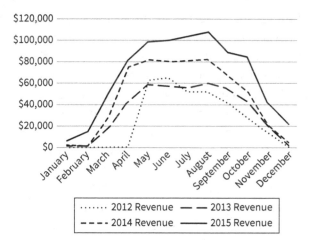

Figure 11.3. Chocolate Moose revenue by month.

needed to generate strategic growth recommendations that would avert the end of the iconic ice cream shop in this college town.

Analyzing the SWOT Elements of the Chocolate Moose

To generate strategic solutions to address their growth concerns, the Chocolate Moose would be well served to begin by completing a SWOT analysis. To illustrate the process of conducting the analysis, let us go through the steps described earlier in the chapter and apply them to the ice cream shop.

Step 1: List and evaluate SWOT elements. In this first step, we look to define the company's internal strengths and weaknesses and external threats and opportunities. A deeper look at the Chocolate Moose's current resources reveals strengths in its local brand recognition and customer loyalty built through years of operation in the Bloomington community, along with a finely tuned production process for homemade ice cream. Physical space limitations imposed by their current location, however, have led to weaknesses in the lack of patronage seating and capacity constraints.

In scanning the external environment, we see there are opportunities for the ice cream store to expand geographically since local and regional demand is not yet saturated, or through distribution channels by exploring partnerships with local wholesalers. The major threats to the Chocolate Moose stem from the changing consumption habits of consumers in search of healthier treats, large retailers offering substitute products at cheaper prices, and the anticipated loss of foot traffic from a pending construction project near its current location.

Step 2: Analyze and rank factors within each category. Armed with a well-structured list of SWOT factors, we turn our attention to ranking each factor based on its relative impact or potential impact on the business. For the Chocolate Moose, with the plethora of store options for local patrons to select from when choosing ice cream, it truly is the strength of their brand that has the most significant impact on the success of the shop, while the most significant burden is the capacity constraints on production. The most significant threat is the anticipated reduction in foot traffic caused by an anticipated construction project, and the chance to establish more meaningful relationships with local wholesalers represents the most impactful opportunity to the shop's current business performance.

Step 3: Combine categories to identify actions and options that link internal and external factors. Once we have ranked factors in each category, we then begin to match factors in each quadrant to develop actionable strategies that link internal and external factors. For example, if we leverage the shop's loyal customer base to expand locally, it is reasonable to propose that the Chocolate Moose either open a new store or pop-up location in Bloomington to meet its local fan base at additional points of purchase.

Step 4: Look at all actions and options and use them to inform overall strategic decisions. The completed analysis presented in Table 11.2 is an integrative view of how the ice cream shop's external environment combines with its resources and capabilities to provide for actionable strategies that can assist the shop in growing its business.

Using insights generated from the SWOT analysis, it is clear that the shop would be well served to expand its retail footprint by

Table 11.2 Integrative SWOT Analysis for the Chocolate Moose

	Strengths	Weaknesses
	S1. Brand recognition	W1. Limited production
	S2. Homemade	capacity
	production	W2. Seasonal store
	S3. Loyal customer base	operations
		W3. Lack of patronage
		seating
Opportunities	**SO Strategies:**	**WO Strategies:**
O1. Area retailers looking for genuine local products to feature	1. (S3, O3) **Invest in a traveling ice cream shop to position at local events**	1. (W2, O2) Pursue market entry in warmer climate
O2. Select other cities have limited ice cream offering that does not satisfy demand	2. (S2, O1) Develop organic homemade ice cream for local organic foods store	2. (W1, O1) Codevelop ice cream line with local grocer
O3. The local ice cream market is not yet saturated	3. (S1, O3) Sponsor Little League Baseball team in Bloomington to increase awareness	2. (W3, O3) **Expand current store location with customer seating area**
Threats	**ST Strategies:**	**WT Strategies:**
T1. Year-long city street construction	1. (T1, S3) Place signage on street to alert passersby	1. (T1, W2) Offer promotions during winter months to drive volume off-peak
T2. Volume discounts offered by national brands	2. (T3, S2) Develop low-fat, low-sugar homemade ice cream offerings	2. (T2, W2) Advertise limited availability to increase customer willingness to pay
T3. Consumer trend toward healthier options		

Note: The numbers following each strategic action reflect the interrelationship between identified prioritized factors in the development of a particular strategy.

adding both a new storefront and mobile food truck. The strength of the Chocolate Moose brand is being held back solely by constraints in production and distribution capabilities, and any excess capacity generated by the new store location could easily be consumed by bringing the Chocolate Moose product closer to the customer at one of Bloomington's many outdoor summertime events.

To deliver on this strategic choice, the Chocolate Moose did indeed choose to locate a second store in the downtown area of the neighboring community of Nashville, Indiana. The two stores were a mere twenty miles apart, and the strength of the brand translated easily to the new location. Within a week of opening, sales in the second location rivaled the flagship store back in Bloomington.

Additionally, the Chocolate Moose started a social gathering called "Food Truck Fridays." Every Friday, from April to October, Bloomingtonians now gather at lunchtime to enjoy the best local mobile food vendors along with great live music, airbrush tattoos, and, of course, the Chocolate Moose's signature homemade ice cream. Within a season of opening the second store and initiating mobile truck service, the Chocolate Moose had secured its future and remains a fixture in the local Bloomington community.

12
Root-Cause Analysis

Purpose and Objective

A root-cause analysis is used to identify the initiating, or root, of a causal chain that leads to the undesirable outcome observed. It is useful in helping managers and practitioners to focus their problem-solving efforts on providing remedies to issues that actually prevent the undesirable outcome from recurring. Failure to identify the root cause of a problem often leads to time spent on removing causal factors, which can alleviate the symptoms of a problem yet may not prevent recurrence with full certainty.

Underlying Theory

While earlier traces of root-cause analysis can be found in the field of medicine, the application of this analytical tool in a business context is attributed to Sakichi Toyada, the founder of Toyota Motor Corporation. The analysis was born out of the work of quality management, which began in Japan at the turn of the twentieth century. In the 1980s, W. Edwards Deming would later help U.S. companies such as Motorola and General Electric codify practices such as Six Sigma and Lean processing, which relied heavily on his famous Fourteen Points[1] and the core principles he learned while working with the Japanese industrialists on quality matters.

One of the underlying ideas behind root-cause analysis is the belief that problems can only be eradicated by attempting to address their root cause, as opposed to addressing its more easily identifiable symptom. As engineers diagnosed the causes of quality issues at

Toyota, it became evident that all problems arose from root causes, and if resolutions were put in place to address these root causes, the problem would be permanently solved. These solutions were deemed "high-quality solutions." Alternatively, if the focus of resolution remained on alleviating symptoms of the problem, negative outcomes would persist after only being alleviated temporarily.

Core Idea

The core idea behind root-cause analysis is to begin with the expressed pain point, challenge, or observed negative outcome and decompose its causes by employing a method called "the five whys." By asking "why" five times or until the root cause of a problem is found, an investigative roadmap is created to systematically identify the deepest issue in a causal chain that can be resolved. An example of a basic root-cause analysis is provided in Figure 12.1.

In practice, the decomposition of complex business problems requires multiple five-whys tests, which can be combined into a hierarchical structure called an issue tree. Typically, issue trees are developed in the diagnosis phase and serve as the investigative roadmap in search of root-cause identification. Causal factors are researched,

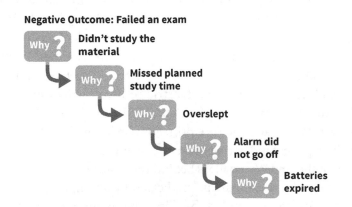

Figure 12.1. Example of root-cause analysis.

and by process of elimination, a source that significantly contributes to the negative or undesirable outcome can be confirmed.

Process

1. Identify the negative or undesirable business outcome of interest.
2. Brainstorm possible causes.
3. Decompose causal factors using the five-whys method.
4. Collect and analyze data to confirm or refute each factor's influence on the undesirable outcome.
5. Choose a root-causal factor that contributes significantly to the negative or undesirable outcome as the key strategic question to be resolved.

Insight or Value Created

The main benefit of root-cause analysis lies in its ability to focus the strategic problem solver on resolving issues that prevent the recurrence of undesirable outcomes, rather than those that merely provide temporary relief from their negative impacts.

Additionally, this analysis provides an opportunity to uncover the causal effects between issues associated with complex business problems and, in so doing, provide clarity and structure to inherently ambiguous problems.

Root-cause analysis also provides a mechanism to sort through the myriad contributing factors, prioritize based on casual relationships, and arrive at a key question that is focused on preventing recurrence.

Risks and Limitations

One potential pitfall when performing root-cause analysis is the lack of logical thinking about the cause-and-effect relationship between events. An example may illustrate this point. Suppose an automotive manufacturer stated that there had been an increase in the number of U.S. car sales during the previous year and attributed the increase to an increase in the number of functioning dealerships. Yet had there not been an increase in the number of car buyers the previous year, the number of actual cars sold would not have been higher. Therefore, while dealerships are necessary for car sales, they would not be the only reason for an increase in sales.

Another possible pitfall is the inability to recognize multiple root causes contributing to the recurrence of an undesirable outcome. Confirming the existence of a root cause is necessary but may not be sufficient in eradicating the problem. Therefore, it becomes imperative that root-cause analysis is inclusive of all possible causal factors and that resolutions are taken for each factor that is found to have contributed.

Case Illustration: DISH Network

Context

Charlie Ergen is the cofounder and chairman of the satellite TV provider DISH Network. The company's core business remains delivery of broadcast television to residential customers, primarily in the United States. The DISH Network Corporation (NASDAQ: DISH) is a Fortune 250 company, and as of November 2016, the company provided services to 13.7 million television and 580,000 broadband subscribers.

In the mid-2000s, Ergen commissioned his teams to take a critical look at all of DISH's varied businesses to determine the best path forward for maintaining a highly diversified yet coordinated portfolio. Further analysis would be required to determine where each business may be vulnerable to market forces and external competitive threat if DISH hoped to fortify and grow a truly diversified portfolio consisting of businesses, each with its own set of challenges.

Of particular concern to Ergen was the threat posed by the recent success of online video and original content creators such as Netflix and Hulu.

Getting to the Root Cause of the Threat from Online Providers

Root-cause analysis would be particularly helpful to Ergen to ensure DISH focuses on addressing the underlying issues contributing to the significant threat posed by online providers. To illustrate the process of conducting this analysis, let us go through the steps described earlier in the chapter and apply them to this scenario.

Step 1: Identify the negative or undesirable business outcome of interest. Faced with the prospect of residential customers moving more toward online providers for movie consumption, DISH needs to determine what assets and capabilities would be necessary for the company to compete effectively with these new market entrants. DISH could start this exploration of root cause by asking the question, "Why do we risk losing market share to online video retailers?"

Step 2: Brainstorm possible causes. From this initial question, we could brainstorm possible reasons that DISH may lose market share as any of the following reasons:

- Inability to advertise effectively
- Inability to offer service at a competitive price
- Inability to distribute online content
- Inability to offer an attractive product
- Inability to provide customer support for online content

Step 3: Decompose causal factors using the five-whys method. Building on this list of initial reasons that DISH may not be competitive in the online market, we seek to decompose each of these reasons by asking ourselves "why?" For example, why might DISH not have effective advertising campaigns for online viewers? Perhaps it is because either their advertising message has not evolved to attract this different customer segment or their advertising isn't being seen by enough online viewers to attract new customers. A full decomposition of each of the possible reasons articulated in step 2 is provided next.

- Our advertising is not effective
  - We have the wrong message
  - Our message is not being seen by our core audience
- Our pricing is not competitive
  - Our pricing structure is too generic
  - Our competitors are taking cost leadership positions
  - Our pricing structure is not responsive to market conditions
- We lack operational support for our product
  - We are not staffed to keep up with service demand
  - We are not effective in addressing service requests
- We lack the proper distribution channel(s)
  - Our satellite service coverage is too limited
  - Our service is not in enough residential homes
- We lack an attractive product
  - Our selection is limited
    - We lack timeless classics
    - We lack specific genres
      - We lack a comedy movie catalog
      - We lack a horror movie catalog
      - We lack a documentary movie catalog
      - We lack an action movie catalog
    - We lack new releases
      - We lack exclusive access with film studios
  - We lack original content creation capabilities

Step 4: Collect and analyze data to confirm or refute each factor's influence on the undesirable outcome. To confirm or refute each factor's influence on DISH's inability to compete with online retailers, it would be beneficial for them to hear directly from DISH's current and potential online customers. Typically, this primary data can be gathered either through a customer survey or focus group.

Step 5: Choose a root-causal factor that contributes significantly to the negative or undesirable outcome as the key strategic question to be resolved. After analyzing the questions elicited from a customer survey, the DISH team was able to generate the insight that its lack of accessibility to newly released movies was one of the most prominent disadvantages and would continue to hinder its competitiveness in the online video business. Further, it was determined that rather than attempt to broker exclusive rights privileges with film studios (which were numerous and would take years to develop), the most expeditious path forward would be to look to acquire the capability by seeking to purchase a company that had already secured these privileges.

We will return to this example in a later chapter to see how DISH Network tested this hypothesis before confirming its choice to make a market acquisition to secure access to new-release movies.

13
S-Curve Analysis

Purpose and Objective

The purpose of an S-curve analysis is to understand and interpret the evolution of a market, product, or technology so as to make informed strategic decisions about where value may be created now and in the future.

S-curves map out the evolution of a market, product, or technology, from its relatively slow emergence, to the point where it begins to grow and growth accelerates, to the point where the market becomes saturated and growth begins to slow and even decline.

Historically, many markets, products, and technologies have followed an S-curve trajectory; therefore, we can expect a similar cycle to repeat itself with current and future markets, products, or technologies. This means that we can use the S-curve concept to assess current markets, products, or technologies and make strategic decisions that factor in such assessments.

Underlying Theory

Logistic functions, which tend to look like a flattened "S" shape, have been found in many different fields and domains of research. One area to which the notion of S-curves is particularly salient in the context of strategy is the study of technological change. Dating back to work as far back as the 1930s,[1] early research studied the diffusion of new technologies like household appliances and color televisions, finding the characteristic initial slow growth when the technology is first introduced, followed by rapidly accelerating growth and a much steeper rate of diffusion when a larger share of the market warms up to the technology, followed by maturity when growth slows again and eventually stops.

As described elsewhere,[2] the evolution of S-curve analysis in the area of strategy accelerated when Levitt[3] introduced the product lifecycle (PLC). Rather than the speed of adoption, newer conceptions of the PLC model sales volume as a function of time, proposing five stages in the "typical" PLC:

1. *Introduction.* A new product or service is introduced in the market and innovators and early adopting customers who are initially unfamiliar with the product make initial purchases.
2. *Growth.* Sales explode as mainstream customers become familiar with the product or service and buy it, and prices fall as firms manage to attain experience and economies of scale and distribution channels are established.
3. *Shakeout.* The initial success of the product or service attracted competitors, yet growth starts to taper off as demand reaches saturation levels. Firms focus on differentiation or cost leadership relative to competitors rather than push the category as a whole; rivalry intensifies with a number of losing firms backing out.
4. *Maturity.* Demand mainly takes the form of replacement purchases, growth slows to a halt, and those having survived the shakeout compete for market share, often leading to a price war.
5. *Decline.* Growth becomes negative as the market is completely saturated; the threat of substitution is real and can set off new PLCs for superior novel products or services, excess capacity leads to inventory being sold at discounted prices, and firms come up with exit strategies and end-game strategies.

S-curve analysis has been criticized for being overly *simplistic*, for underestimating the potential for *product revivals*, and for downplaying the fact that in current times the different phases and activities that make up the PLC may be performed by *different firms along the value chain*—entrepreneurial startups, for example, mainly focusing on developing new products, introducing them to the market, and then "selling out" to larger partners at the growth stage. That being said, S-curve analysis can be credited for shattering the strategic myopia that used to exist among many traditional businesses toward technological discontinuities and change.

Core Idea

Scholars have long observed that markets, products, and technologies tend to progress along well-defined sigmoid or S-curves. Early in the life of a market, product, or technology, businesses experiment with new options, and only a small group of customers (early adopters) are willing to risk buying and using new products or technologies. Performance of various attributes of interest may be lacking— quality may be low, the product may be too large, the performance may be slow, etc. Over time, as experimentation continues, performance improves and growth in demand (for the product, technology, or market interaction) increases and accelerates. At this time, new firms may enter in an attempt to grab a piece of the action. A dominant design or perspective may emerge, resulting in many firms providing similar offerings and features. Eventually, markets become saturated and growth slows. When this happens there may be a shakeout among competitors, with a small number of firms retaining a significant market share in a slow or declining market.

Eventually a new market, product, or technology may emerge to challenge and replace the old one, thereby potentially jumpstarting a new S-curve. When something new arises, it usually takes time to catch on, as the product or technology is refined and as the market takes time to get used to something new. However, new products or technologies eventually emerge and grow, thereby replacing old ones and sometimes making them obsolete (think typewriters, fax machines, travel agents, newspaper classifieds, etc.).

Table 13.1 Firms and Related S-Curves

Examples of Existing Firms That Jumped to a New S-Curve	Examples of Firms That Failed to Jump to a New S-Curve	Examples of Startup Firms That Created a New S-Curve
Netflix: Physical DVDs to video streaming	**Kodak:** Film base photography to digital photography	**E-bay:** Online auctions to replace physical auctions and newspaper classifieds
TED: Annual conferences to broad online knowledge sharing	**Nokia:** Feature phones to smartphones	**Wikipedia:** Online, crowdsourced content to replace published encyclopedias
Kelley: In-class to online graduate education	**Blockbuster:** Physical DVDs to video streaming	**Tesla:** Attempting to create a new S-curve for electric vehicles to replace combustion engines

This is a natural evolution process. It cannot be avoided or reversed. A firm can endeavor to create a portfolio of new initiatives that might produce or leverage a new market, product, or technology such that they can participate in emerging S-curves as they hit the accelerating growth phase. One of the key roles of managers is to invest resources in a manner that produces new S-curves to replace declining ones so as to keep a firm viable for a longer time. Table 13.1 provides examples of firms that jumped to a new S-curve, those that failed to do, and ventures that created a new S-curve.

Depiction

Figure 13.1 shows the different phases of product, technology, or market evolution and the associated growth rate with each phase. It also highlights that a challenge or opportunity emerges when an existing S-curve is in the mature phase, as this is when it is ripe to create a new S-curve.

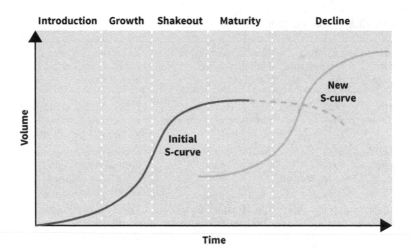

Figure 13.1. S-curve tool for assessing adoption and growth of new products, technologies, or markets.

Process

1. Identify where a firm's existing markets, products, or technologies are on the S-curve. Are they in the introduction, growth, shakeout, mature, or decline phase?
2. Use this as a basis to inform strategic options for that market, product, or technology:
   a. If in the introduction phase, the strategy should focus on facilitating widespread adoption, that is, crossing the chasm from early adopters to mainstream adapters.[4]
   b. If in the growth phase, the strategy may focus on capturing new customers and striving to ensure that the focal firm's products, technologies, or ways of operating become the standard for the industry.
   c. If in the shakeout phase, then the value proposition (low-cost or clear differentiation) may be more important than ever, as customers tend to have choices and be well educated on alternatives; hence, they make well-informed decisions and firms with good value propositions should survive

the shakeout. At this point, a key consideration may also be investing in new markets, technologies, or products to create a new S-curve.

d. If in the mature phase, the firms with entrenched positions and large economies of scale are likely to succeed. This stage requires that managers carefully and cautiously manage current operations so as to maximize efficiencies and keep costs down, but also invest heavily in a new portfolio of markets, technologies, or products to create or find a new S-curve.

e. If in the decline stage, managers generally have four options: (1) exit—bankruptcy or liquidation, (2) harvest—reduce investment and just maximize cash flow, (3) maintain—continue supporting the business at a reasonable level, or (4) consolidate—buy rivals to establish a stronger position. Whichever of these options one chooses, if the firm is to be around long term, it probably needs investments in new markets, technologies, or products to create new growth opportunities.

3. Assess how rapidly the markets, products, or technologies in the focal industry are changing and how quickly the focal market, product, or technology will move through the different phases. Use this as a basis to understand how long current markets, products, or technologies may provide sustainable revenue streams.

4. View the array of markets, products, or technologies within a business as a portfolio and use a portfolio perspective in making strategic decisions about where to play and how to win.

5. Consider competitor positions with respect to (a) their current market, product, or technology portfolio and the associated S-curves and (b) the investments they are making in new markets, technologies, or products.

Insight or Value Created

The S-curve perspective makes managers and practitioners aware of the dynamism affecting their businesses. It highlights how the markets, technologies, or products that a firm depends on today may not be the ones that make it successful in the future. It prompts managers and practitioners to carefully consider the impact of innovation and change on their business—how innovation can be leveraged as a source of advantage but also how the innovation of others (existing firms and startups) could be the source of their demise.

This kind of analysis allows managers to understand how long they may generate value from their existing portfolio of markets, technologies, and products and helps highlight what strategic philosophy is required for each, depending on where it is positioned along the S-curve.

Risks and Limitations

Not all markets, technologies, or products follow an S-curve trajectory. Therefore, there may be times where managers or practitioners depend on an S-curve to make projections or decide on strategic options and they end up getting things very wrong.

Even though many markets, technologies, and products follow an S-curve trajectory, knowing how long each phase will last is very difficult. It is very challenging to predict how long it may take for a product to shift from introduction to growth or how long the growth phase may last until a shakeout occurs. Therefore, even though the S-curve perspective may offer suggestions about what may happen in the future, getting the timing right to act on those suggestions can be very problematic.

Case Illustration: Spotify

Context

Spotify, the music streaming service that was founded in 2006 by Daniel Ek and Martin Lorentzon, allows users to stream music, videos, and podcasts online through Spotify's website or software application. When the service first launched in 2008, it was entering an extremely challenging industry context. The big record labels controlled almost all of the desirable music content, and they had strong relationships with established distribution channels (music retailers) and emerging new channels (Apple iTunes). However, the technological options used to distribute music and other audio content were changing, and this change had the potential to open up opportunities for new entrants. Analyzing and assessing this could provide the Spotify founders with a clearer perspective of the opportunity they were pursuing. Hence, they could use S-curve analysis to understand key elements of the opportunity and to inform their decisions about how to exploit this opportunity.

Understanding and Analyzing an Industry in Transformation

Step 1: Identify where a firm's existing markets, products, or technologies are on the S-curve. Are they in the introduction, growth, shakeout, mature, or decline phase? For the Spotify founders, this could entail mapping the evolution of the music distribution industry as it transitioned from vinyl records, to cassette tapes, to compact discs, and then to digital audio files. Assessing how long it took for each of these music distribution options to take hold, and how long each was dominant, might provide insight into how quickly a new distribution option such as streaming might take hold. In doing this, the founders could assess where they thought the market for compact discs (mature) and the market for digital audio files (growth) were in 2008. This would give them an idea of what they were up against as they launched Spotify as a music streaming service.

Step 2: Use this as a basis to inform strategic options for that market, product, or technology. The Spotify founders would assess that the market for music streaming was still in the introduction phase, after a few false starts in the early days of the internet. Hence, their challenge in 2008 was to facilitate widespread adoption of streaming as a primary means to listen to music, thereby crossing the chasm from a few early adopters of music streaming to mainstream adoption, where everyone began to see it as a viable option. Their analysis would also allow them to see that CD distribution at that time was in a mature phase, but digital downloads were in a growth phase. This would help them understand that competitors in the digital downloads business (e.g., Apple iTunes) would be focused on capturing new customers and striving to ensure that the iTunes platform became the standard for the industry.

Step 3: Assess how rapidly the markets, products, or technologies in the focal industry are changing and how quickly the focal market, product, or technology will move through the different phases. Use this as a basis to understand how long current markets, products, or technologies may provide sustainable revenue streams. The Spotify founders would more systematically assess the digital downloads market. They could study how fast the market was growing and examine the pain points of customers in this market to assess how they might encourage current customers to adopt a new distribution technology (streaming).

Step 4: View the array of markets, products, or technologies within a business as a portfolio and use a portfolio perspective in making strategic decisions about where to play and how to win. In this case, because Spotify was a startup venture, they didn't have a broad array of products.

Step 5: Consider competitor positions with respect to (a) their current market, product, or technology portfolio and the associated S-curves and (b) the investments they are making in new markets, technologies, or products. As the founders of Spotify studied one of their strongest competitors, Apple, they would realize that Apple had a portfolio of product types that were each at different phases of the respective S-curve; in 2008, desktop and laptop computers (iMacs) were in the mature phase, iPods were in the shakeout phase, iPhones and iTunes were still in the growth phase, and iPads were in the introduction phase. This wide product portfolio, with products in each phase of the S-curve, would make Apple a formidable competitor and Spotify would need to be very focused with its value proposition to compete with Apple. In addition to this, the founders would note

Table 13.2 Summary of Competitor Insights Generated by the S-Curve Analysis

	Introduction	Growth	Shakeout	Maturity	Decline
Focal Firm					
Spotify	Streaming service				
Competitors					
Apple	iPad	iPhone iTunes	iPod	iMac	
Pandora	Streaming service				
Sony					Compact discs

that Pandora was in a very similar position to Spotify on the S-curve, with a single music streaming service as the core offering of the company. The competitor insights generated by the S-curve analysis are reflected in Table 13.2.

All of this information would be useful for the Spotify founders as they considered their product development, marketing, and competitive challenges in the early phases of the venture. It points to the need to generate an understanding of the interest in a largely unknown service (music streaming) and to develop different approaches to compete with competitors with very different product portfolios (Apple versus Pandora).

14
Value Chain Analysis

Purpose and Objective

Value chain analysis (VCA) aids the strategist in mapping and understanding a firm's (potential) sources of competitive advantage by decomposing the firm into strategically important activities. VCA also provides a basis to structure a firm's activities to deliver on a desired form of competitive advantage. Viewing the firm as an aggregate of interlinked value-adding activities and placing them in the context of a broader value chain helps to understand each activity's impact on both cost and revenue potential, and structure a firm to deliver on its ultimate value proposition. As such, VCA can be used to help the firm achieve an optimal allocation of resources. VCA is often used as the basis for making decisions regarding the potential outsourcing of activities, as VCA helps understand and evaluate which activities contribute most substantially to a firm's competitive advantage and which do not.

Underlying Theory

VCA's theoretical basis lies in Michael Porter's 1985 book *Competitive Advantage.*[1] To understand the underlying theoretical perspectives of VCA, it is helpful to focus on two of its important distinguishing characteristics. First, VCA is essentially concerned with *identifying sources of competitive advantage*. This approach is rooted in microeconomics, in which the firm is viewed as a collection of discrete yet related activities, some of which are not traded in external markets.[2] As Hergert and Morris[3] explain, those activities that are not traded in external markets can generate rents for the firm and form a distinguishing characteristic from rivals. Strategists should identify and pay close attention to those activities that are the actual (or potential) source of such advantages.

A second important distinguishing characteristic of VCA that helps to uncover its theoretical foundation is Porter's formulation of *generic strategies* that firms can follow to optimize the activities in their value chain. Aiming to resolve the conundrum that both firms with a large market share and those with a low market share could be very profitable (in fact, often more so than those in the middle), Porter proposed that successful firms with large market share tend to focus on cost leadership through economies of efficiency and scale, and those with a small market share focus on differentiation into profitable market niches. That is, a *cost leadership strategy* seeks to create the same or similar value for customers by delivering products or services at a lower cost than competitors, enabling the firm to offer lower prices to customers. A *differentiation strategy*, in contrast, seeks to create higher value for customers than the value that competitors create by delivering products or services with unique features while keeping costs at the same or similar levels.[4] Porter's work on generic strategies and how they are implemented in the value chain was born from a shift in strategy thinking that was occurring at the time. The *atomistic view of strategy* that had prevailed in strategy literature for a long time essentially considered each firm to be unique in every respect.[5] The new view that replaced the atomistic view, and which was supported by Porter's work on VCA, instead was centered on the recognition of commonalities between groups of firms following similar strategies within an industry, which provided an intermediate perspective between viewing industries as wholes and considering each firm separately.[6]

VCA is a way to analyze and understand the structuring of activities in firms that pursue these different generic strategies of differentiation or cost leadership. It essentially examines what sequence of activities firms engage in to develop low-cost or highly differentiated outputs.

Core Idea

A fundamental notion in VCA is that products/services gain value as they pass through the vertical stream of production within the firm. When the created value exceeds the cost of every activity that the firm must perform to transform the product or service into a final sale, it generates a profit.[7]

The value chain represents the internal activities a firm engages in when transforming inputs into outputs. *Primary activities* are those activities that are directly tied to the initial taking of inputs, the subsequent converting of products, and the ultimate delivery of outputs to the customers. Primary activities include:

- *Inbound logistics*—inventory management, warehousing, and handling
- *Operations*—the actual transformation of inputs into outputs
- *Outbound logistics*—distribution channels, shipping, and delivery
- *Marketing and sales*—marketing communications and pricing
- *Service*—pre- and postsale support[8]

Support activities play an auxiliary role to the primary activities. While they are not directly tied to the transformation of the core product or service, they are no less important than the primary activities. Support activities include:

- *Technology*—research and development, information and communications technology, and engineering
- *Human resource management*—hiring, promotion, incentive systems, and training
- *Infrastructure*—administrative support, physical infrastructure, and stakeholder relations[9]

Competitive advantage can be achieved both by individual activities themselves and through joint optimization of interdependent activities. Such a joint optimization of interdependencies is typically extremely hard to develop and sustain, and even harder for other firms to copy, and hence an important source of competitive advantage.

VCA places firms' internal capabilities in the context of the external competitive environment. As such, one very important application of VCA pertains to decisions regarding *strategic outsourcing*. The strategic outsourcing (or insourcing) of activities that are not (or are potentially) important drivers of competitive advantage critically hinge on an in-depth understanding of a firm's value chain. A well-known illustration of the radically different strategies companies can pursue regarding their positioning within the value chain is the difference between Ecco's and Nike's approaches toward producing and selling footwear. Ecco's fully vertically integrated value chain approach ("From cow to customer") involves everything from initial leather production in tanneries, to inbound logistics and operations, to eventual sales and marketing. Nike, in contrast, long ago decided to outsource its procurement of raw materials and manufacturing of footwear and apparel to international third parties, even while footwear and apparel together constitute over 85% of Nike's revenue.

The model[10] reflected in Table 14.1 provides a useful way to frame strategic outsourcing decisions, drawing on the critical VCA-based

Table 14.1 Framing Strategic Outsourcing Decisions

		Relative Capability Position	
		Less Capable	*More Capable*
Contribution to Competitive Advantage	*Critical*	Invest to perform internally or outsource	Perform internally and develop
	Not critical	Outsource	Outsource or maintain

insight of the activity's contribution to competitive advantage and the degree to which the firm is more or less capable than others in performing the activity. At the two extremes, an activity that is not critical to the firm's competitive advantage and for which the firm has a weak relative capability position is likely best outsourced; an activity that is critical to the firm's competitive position and which the firm is better able to perform than others is likely best performed internally as part of the firm's value chain, and possibly further developed.

Depiction

The value chain can be depicted as a series of activities, shown in Figure 14.1.[11] This figure shows that products/services gain value as they pass through the vertical stream of production within the firm, from inbound logistics, to operations, to outbound logistics, to sales and marketing, to aftersales service. These are supported by key support activities such as infrastructure, technology, and human resources.

Process

1. Define the focal company's boundaries and define its strategic business units. In doing this, it is important to do so

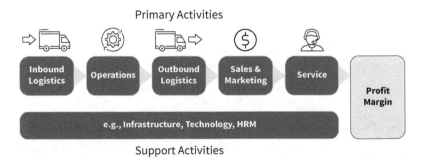

Figure 14.1. Value chain analysis tool for analyzing primary and support activities for generating value within a firm.

consistently with unit operations, which may or may not overlap with organizational charts.

2. Analyze the wider vertical process involved in converting raw materials into final sales and service, and the focal company's position in it.

3. Identify the company's key activities, both the primary activities along each component of the value chain (inbound logistics, operations, etc.) and the support activities.

4. Conduct a cost analysis of each of the activities identified by attempting to isolate and break down cost drivers specific to each activity.

5. Conduct an analysis of the activities' relative value. This can be tricky since customers typically pay for a final product, not the intermediate activities that led to its production or specific individual features. Still, in performing in-depth customer research, one can isolate specific aspects of the final product or service and request feedback on how important it is to customers' purchasing decisions and how satisfied they are with it.

6. Analyze the firm's relative capability position regarding key activities by benchmarking horizontally to competitors doing similar activities.

7. Analyze key interdependencies between different activities either in terms of their cost or in terms of their added value.

8. Evaluate the firm's value chain by reviewing key activities in light of their cost (step 4), relative value (step 5), the firm's relative capability position regarding them (step 6), and their interdependencies (step 7).

9. Identify opportunities for optimization through investing, divesting, developing, or outsourcing.

Insight or Value Created

A VCA provides perspective and insight on the many ways all of a company's activities, independently and jointly, relate to overall profit and competitive advantages. As such, it is a very useful tool to assess the significance of specific firm activities, often being an important analytical input into decisions regarding activity structuring, resource allocation, and the potential in- or outsourcing of activities.

At the same time, VCA prompts managers to think about the way their firm is positioned in the overall vertical process by which raw materials are transformed into end products. As such, VCA is very useful to gain an understanding of the company's competitive position relative to key customers and suppliers.[12]

Risks and Limitations

Despite its many strengths, VCA has a number of weaknesses. First, it is notoriously hard to accurately determine the value of each (sub) activity that leads to the sale of a final product or service.[13] That is, while the central notion of VCA is that a profit can be generated through a positive difference between added value and cost as a product or service passes through the vertical stream of production within the firm, it is hard to accurately assess the perceived value of each activity relative to its cost. Customers typically are unaware or indifferent to the intermediate activities that led to the final configuration of their product, making assessing each intermediate activity's relative contribution to overall customer value hard to assess.

Second, while the complex interdependencies between various value-adding activities are central to VCA, the value generated by joint optimization and coordination efficiencies are hard to quantify. Accounting systems used in firms typically assume independence of subunits;[14] hence, modeling the value relative to cost of well- (or poorly) designed interdependencies is extremely challenging.

A third and more general critique of VCA is that it may be seen to "place the customer last." That is, in the archetype VCA, the customer remains at the receiving end of the value chain. This might work well for the efficient production and delivery of undifferentiated products. However, as Merchant[15] perhaps claimed most forcefully, the key to thriving in our current era lies in distinctiveness and customized products. Social media and other ICTs are increasingly enabling a true "placing the customer first" model. In fact, in many industries firms have direct and immediate contact with (potential) end-users, making potential customers critical contributors to the identification of market needs and the early development and testing of prototype products. Many companies today, in settings ranging from fashion and furniture to technology and services, are essentially reversing the value chain by having customers dictate what they want, how they want it, and when they want it. These companies subsequently produce only what has been ordered, reversing the value chain to produce and assemble only what has already been sold.[16] Such novel ways of production establish important boundary conditions to the universal application of traditional VCA across different products and markets.

Case Illustration: Netflix

Context

Let us return to Netflix to illustrate VCA. Recall that the market for online video was going through some major disruption from 2018 onward. The market was rapidly growing and Netflix was doing well, but some formidable competitors were chomping at the bit to get a piece of the pie, and Netflix was starting to face some significant threats.

Assessing the Value Chain of Entertainment Streaming

Step 1: Define the focal company's boundaries and define its strategic business units. For a well-known company like Netflix, plenty of (online) sources document the company's layout. We won't rehash that here but will rather unpack that structure in step 3 in a way that it is directly relevant to the tool in question.

Step 2: Analyze the wider vertical process involved in converting raw materials into final sales and service, and the focal company's position in it. The wider vertical process whereby "raw materials" are transformed into outputs in this industry would look something like what is depicted in Figure 14.2. That is, content is first created (i.e., movies and series are written, shot, and produced), then either licensed to someone else for further use or moved internally (in the case of a company producing its own original content) to the next phase of production. Key corporate functions in the case of Netflix are content aggregation on its servers and developing its platform to a user-friendly environment that uses smart algorithms to get to know customers' preferences. The finished product—the Netflix online library of content—is then retailed to customers through the sale of subscriptions. Activated accounts are fulfilled by ensuring users have full access to the content. Content is made available through data that flows to end-users through internet service providers (ISPs). Customers can then access the content on smart devices through the ISPs. The key activities of Netflix are summarized in Figure 14.2.

Key activities	Performed by	
Raw material production (content creation)	Netflix Disney, AMC, etc.	UPSTREAM
Wholesale (licensing)	Netflix Disney, AMC, etc.	
Transportation		
Corporate functions (content aggregation)	Netflix	
Finished products (content: series, films)	Netflix	
Retail (streaming subscription service)	Netflix	
Fulfillment (content serving)	Netflix	
Distribution (data)	Internet Service Providers	DOWNSTREAM
Use phase/ service (content consumption)	iPhone (Apple), smart TVs (Samsung, etc.), Roku	

Figure 14.2. Assessing the key activities performed by Netflix versus others.

Step 3: Identify the company's key activities, both the primary activities along each component of the value chain (inbound logistics, operations, etc.) and the support activities. In the case of Netflix, one can at a high level demarcate the following primary and secondary activities:

- *Inbound logistics.* Traditionally, back when Netflix relied mainly on others to produce the content of its entertainment portfolio, inbound logistics meant negotiating with content producers and obtaining licenses for showing content developed by others. For the increasing share of content that Netflix had produced itself, one way to think about inbound logistics is in terms of co-ordinating and assembling production teams, a cast, a director, etc., for producing original content.
- *Operations.* One of the main value-adds that Netflix offers is content aggregation: making its content available in a way that is accessible, inviting, and personalized. Netflix's algorithms for knowing what users like and what they would like to watch next is a huge competitive edge.
- *Outbound logistics.* This covers anything related to getting the finalized content to end-users. For Netflix, this means negotiating with ISPs who in the end have to ensure that the enormous amounts of streaming data reach end-users.
- *Sales and marketing.* For Netflix this covers its outreach and marketing activities, which tend to generally involve a quite casual voice toward customers, social media campaigns, and efforts to get users to become its ambassadors by encouraging viewers to share content with others. It also involves witty and creative projects that tend to go viral (remember the Netflix Socks project?).
- *Service.* Netflix claims, "We promise our customers stellar service," and its somewhat quirky approach to customer service fits that bill. Customer service agents are not bound by a static script they have to read and go through with a customer, and canceling is easy, lowering the risk for people otherwise hesitant to commit to a subscription model.

Netflix's secondary activities are its server infrastructure and technology, human resources, etc. Netflix's corporate culture and infamous vacation policy (which consists of just five words: "There is no policy or tracking") is key to its human resources policy. Netflix is absolutely convinced that working with great people and providing them with the context and freedom to excel leads to great results. Netflix's culture deck, a 124-slide presentation that can be found on jobs.netflix.com/culture, was praised by Facebook COO Sheryl Sandberg as follows: "It may well be the most important document ever to come out of the Valley."

For steps 4 and 5 (*Step 4: Conduct a cost analysis of each of the activities identified by attempting to isolate and break down cost drivers specific to each activity; Step 5: Conduct an analysis of the activities' relative value*), let us zoom in on one specific and interesting activity currently still performed by others: distribution (data).

Historically, acquiring streaming content had always been a challenge for Netflix. With that alleviated through original content production, one of Netflix's challenges was dealing with ISPs. Netflix accounted for 35% of peak internet traffic and delivered over 125 million hours of video per day.[17] This sheer volume of traffic placed a heavy burden on ISPs. Despite Netflix enabling offline viewing and moving servers closer to end-users, Netflix critically relies on ISPs for a sizeable chunk of its user interface and critical user experience. Some of Netflix's competitors, which are telecom companies, had a unique advantage over Netflix, particularly since the Trump administration rolled back the net neutrality rules in the United States. This left ISPs with a suite of tactics (some of them questionable, like throttling or data caps) that could severely hamper Netflix in an oncoming streaming war. According to one source, all three major ISPs had already explored the idea of driving up costs that streaming competitors must pay to access their networks.[18] This then leaves us with an interesting value chain question: should Netflix forward integrate by providing internet services itself? Would that even be possible?

Step 6: Analyze the firm's relative capability position regarding key activities by benchmarking horizontally to competitors doing similar activities. When it comes to data distribution, one could state that on one hand this is critical to Netflix's competitive advantage, but that at the same time, Netflix could not yet offer that service at a level of capability that an existing ISP could. When posing the question of forward integration, note that we are not necessarily talking about establishing a separate physical wire connection into people's homes (even though Alphabet has embarked on such a mission with Google Fiber, which could be a potential alliance partner).

Let us merge steps 7 through 9 (*Step 7: Analyze key interdependencies between different activities either in terms of their cost or in terms of their added value; Step 8: Evaluate the firm's value chain by reviewing key activities in light of their cost [step 4], relative value [step 5], the firm's relative capability position regarding them step [6], and their interdependencies [step 7]; Step 9: Identify opportunities for optimization through investing, divesting, developing, or outsourcing*). That is, the question of whether Netflix might possibly want to forward integrate hinges on understanding the interdependencies and costs of each activity, their (potential) added value, and Netflix's relative capability position. At the time of writing, Netflix had yet to make any forward movement in terms of dramatically altering its share of value chain activities. However, competitors vertically integrating (telecom providers also starting streaming services and developing content, movie studios merging with downstream organizations) threatens a component of the value chain that is critical to Netflix's overall value proposition—the user experience—and further vertically integrating itself could be one way to mitigate this threat.

15
Hypothesis Testing

Purpose and Objective

The purpose of hypothesis testing is to provide the decision maker with an efficient mechanism for reducing uncertainty using an inferential procedure to test the credibility of a potential solution to a strategic challenge. Choosing an initial hypothesis about how to solve a problem and limiting data collection and analysis to those data that either defend or reject this hypothesis can be far more efficient than traditional methods of collecting data without purpose and deducing solutions by analyzing relevant data and eliminating irrelevant data along the way.

Underlying Theory

The concept of hypothesis testing was born out of scientific research. In practice, the use of hypothesis testing as a strategic analysis tool was made popular by management consulting firms such as McKinsey & Co. in the mid-twentieth century and further elaborated upon within firms such as Procter & Gamble.

The philosophy behind hypothesis testing is that logically, one can never have enough evidence to definitely prove that something is true. This is because the next bit of evidence to the contrary could prove it false. However, you can have enough evidence to prove definitively that something is *not true* or highly likely to fail. For example, one could never prove that all leopards in the wild have spots, because at some point in the future, we may stumble upon a leopard with stripes instead of spots. However, it is possible for us to prove that not all leopards have spots (after all, we only need to find one example of a leopard without spots). Scientists mitigate the perpetual existence of doubt for their claims using a principle called "reversal of claims," in which they seek to disprove a false claim, thus providing greater assurance that through a process of elimination there is greater confidence in acceptance of a claim that is true. For example, although it may be very challenging for scientists to prove that a particular blood pressure medication regulates blood pressure, it is far easier for them to disprove that the medication does not spike or lower blood pressure.

Given that hypothesis testing provides a mechanism for scientists to deal with uncertainty in the natural world, it is clear to see the utility of this analytical approach in a business context, a discipline in which decisions makers are routinely called upon to make decisions in ambiguous, complex, and often uncertain circumstances without perfect information.

Core Idea

The core idea behind hypothesis testing is to choose from among solution alternatives an initial hypothesis that appears most viable and illuminate all the necessary conditions that need to be tested to build defensible support for the alternative. This is accomplished by asking, "What must be true?" about the chosen alternative for decision makers to be confident in their choice. The collective set of conditions that must be tested can be organized into a hypothesis tree, and subsequent data collection and analysis efforts are focused on generating evidence that either confirms or refutes each of the conditions in the tree.

To generate the list of alternatives to choose a hypothesis from, it is common for strategists to brainstorm the list of possible solutions by employing a method called "the five hows." By asking "how" five times or until the specific actionable step of a solution is identified, a solution roadmap (often referred to as the logic tree) is created to systematically identify the executable strategic actions that can be taken to resolve the business challenge. The more specific the actions are, the more accurate the hypothesis testing tends to be. Once all possible solutions have been enumerated, the strategist uses experience, instinct, and sound judgment to select the most viable alternative to proceed with hypothesis testing. This will naturally feel uncomfortable for those more accustomed to deductive problem-solving techniques, but in practice, it becomes necessary to push beyond this hesitancy to prioritize and test the most viable of alternatives.

Process

The process for utilizing a hypothesis testing approach is as follows:[1]

1. Generate a list of possible solutions to the key challenge being evaluated.
2. Describe the specific delivery actions for each possible solution by asking the "five hows," and organize actions into a logic tree.
3. Using instinct and experience, select an initial hypothesis or "day 1 answer" from the list of possible solutions to test (ideally this should be a strategic possibility that is considered highly favorable).
4. Identify the conditions that must be true for the initial hypothesis to be defensible, and organize conditions into a hypothesis tree.
5. Collect and analyze data in support of proving or disproving each of the conditions in the hypothesis tree.
6. If the hypothesis is disproven, return to step 3 and select a new hypothesis. If the hypothesis is supported, use insights from the data analysis performed earlier to justify the recommendation.

Depiction

Figure 15.1 provides a visual depiction of the hypothesis-testing approach as described in this chapter. It starts on the left with listing the strategic possibilities and how each of those possibilities would be implemented, and then from there, it identifies the "day 1 option"

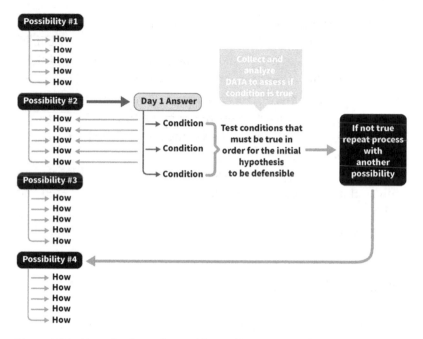

Figure 15.1. Hypothesis testing tool for making strategic choices.

and the conditions that would need to be true for the day 1 option to be viable and defensible. Finally, data is collected and analyzed to assess if those conditions are likely to be true. If not, another possibility is assessed.

Insight or Value Created

The primary benefit of using hypothesis testing in the strategy-making process is that it helps the decision maker define and appropriately direct research and analysis efforts in an attempt to expedite the decision-making process. Instead of gathering topical data without an explicit purpose, hypothesis testing allows for targeted data gathering with the intent of validating very specific conditions related to the proposed solution.

A secondary benefit of this analysis is that the artifacts created by the analysis become highly reusable in justifying or "selling" the recommendation to key stakeholders. Many of the conditions outlined in the hypothesis tree will be the commonly held beliefs regarding the unknowns or risks of a particular course of action. The confirming evidence used to prove the hypothesis often forms the basis of convincing others and alleviating skepticism about the recommendation chosen.

Finally, use of hypothesis testing also leaves a rather explicit audit trail of the logic behind a decision and the data gathered and analyzed. This may be helpful in answering questions regarding what alternatives were also considered and ultimately not chosen.

Risks and Limitations

There are three potential pitfalls of using this analytical approach to derive strategic choice. First, it is possible that by choosing hypotheses that continue to be disproven through analysis, you could in fact exhaust all alternatives and be forced to more traditional methods of deductive problem solving. While this is theoretically possible, it is important to keep in mind that typically strategists work with rather experienced team members whose on-the-job training and judgment are summarily discounted by this argument. In practice, very rarely does a team need to go back to their list of alternatives in the logic tree more than a few times before finding a solution, or set of solutions, that satisfies the key question.

It is this search for a satisfying solution that leads to the second potential risk of this approach—namely, that by not exploring all possible alternatives, the strategist may unintentionally ignore an optimal solution in favor of validation of a satisfying solution. Once again, although there is theoretical justification for this argument, it fails to consider the reality that the marginal cost and extended time of searching for an optimal solution rarely outweigh the incremental benefits of doing so. In most industries the pace of change is so rapid that most strategic decision makers recognize the value in identifying a satisfying solution rapidly, allowing them to quickly move on to the next challenge.

Similar to scientific research, the third potential risk of using hypothesis testing to make decisions is that errors can be made in accepting or rejecting the hypothesis. A Type I error results from rejecting the initial hypothesis when in fact the data gathered and analyzed all support the hypothesized solution. This is far less common than a Type II error, which results from confirming a hypothesis by failing to uncover disconfirming evidence during the research and analysis of the proposed solution. The more comprehensive the hypothesis tree, the less risk there is of a Type II error during the analysis.

Case Illustration: DISH Network

Context

The DISH Network is a satellite TV provider located in Englewood, Colorado. The company's core business is the delivery of broadcast television to residential customers, primarily in the United States. As of November 2016, the company provided services to 13.7 million television and 580,000 broadband subscribers.

In the mid-2000s, the emergent threat posed by the success of online video and original content creators such as Netflix and Hulu weighed heavily on cofounder and chairman Charlie Ergen. In response, DISH made the decision in April of 2011 to acquire the failed Blockbuster LLC video rental chain in a bankruptcy claim for $320 million. The prevailing thought among DISH executives was that not only would the purchase give the company more cross-sale opportunities that could lead to even more robust streaming offerings but also, more important, it would strengthen and fortify its current streaming offering by providing access to new-release movie titles that Blockbuster had previously secured for their numerous retail locations.

Testing the Idea of Acquiring Blockbuster

Hypothesis testing would be particularly helpful to Ergen and his team to ensure the decision to acquire Blockbuster would not only address the acute need to secure access to new-release movie titles but also not result in any unintended negative consequences to the rest of the organization. To illustrate the process of conducting this analysis, let us go through the steps described earlier in the chapter and apply them to this scenario.

Step 1: Generate a list of possible solutions to the key challenge being evaluated. As we saw in Chapter 12 when discussing root-cause analysis, the team at DISH had determined that one of the most significant contributing factors to the unattractiveness of its online offerings was the gap that existed in its product catalog with regard to new-release movie titles. When considering how to close this gap, DISH faced a classic buy versus build decision.

Step 2: Describe the specific delivery actions for each possible solution by asking the "five hows," and organize actions into a logic tree. DISH could "build" that capability organically by establishing relationships and contractual agreements with movie producers such as Universal Studios, MGM, and Paramount. Alternatively, DISH could look to acquire a company that currently possessed the access it sought such as Blockbuster or Netflix.

Step 3: Using instinct and experience, select an initial hypothesis or "day 1 answer" from the list of possible solutions to test. Knowing that DISH ultimately decided to acquire Blockbuster, it is clear that acquisition of the company was the hypothesis executives chose to test.

Step 4: Identify the conditions that must be true for the initial hypothesis to be defensible, and organize conditions into a hypothesis tree. To validate the decision to acquire Blockbuster, it is plausible that executives from DISH likely would have worked to confirm the following conditions were true:

1. Blockbuster still owns its access rights to new movie releases.

2. Blockbuster will create a positive economic return for DISH.
   - Additional value can be created by combining operations.
     - There will be revenue synergies.
     - There will be cost savings from combined operations.
   - DISH is paying a fair price to acquire Blockbuster.
     - Blockbuster has a stable revenue stream.
     - Blockbuster has a modest cost structure.
3. There are no integration barriers that would prevent DISH from realizing a return.
   - There is cultural alignment between both organizations.
     - Leadership team holds common values.
     - Employee work environment is similar.
   - There are no regulatory or legal barriers to acquisition.

Step 5: Collect and analyze data in support of proving or disproving each of the conditions in the hypothesis tree. Collecting and analyzing data for every element of the hypothesis tree can be time consuming and tedious, but by definition, the evidence collected from attempting to prove or disprove the conditions in the tree are essential to confirm the proposed action is viable. What stands out in particular in this hypothesis is the cost structure of Blockbuster and what to do with the 1700 store locations across the United States that DISH would be purchasing in the bankruptcy auction.

Step 6. If the hypothesis is disproven, return to step 3 and select a new hypothesis. If the hypothesis is supported, use insights from the data analysis performed earlier to justify the recommendation. It is certainly possible that DISH intended to leverage Blockbuster's physical presence in marketing campaigns aimed at attracting Blockbuster's customers to DISH's subscription services. However, in the process of making this decision, if the decision markers at DISH felt they could not achieve an orderly liquation of Blockbuster's brick-and-mortar stores, it would have been completely reasonable for them to have rejected this acquisition entirely. In doing so, they would have returned to their list of solutions and chosen another candidate to test by building a new hypothesis tree.

16
Segmentation Analysis

Purpose and Objective

Segmentation analysis provides a means to understand and partition a broad consumer or business market into subgroups of consumers or businesses (called segments), such that a firm can effectively target specific segments rather than the market as a whole. Segments are created based on shared attributes of consumers or businesses such as shared needs, common interests, similar locations, common demographic profiles, etc. Segmenting a market allows a firm's managers to understand and target segments that are most attractive for the firm. Segment attractiveness is based on factors internal and external to a firm. From an internal perspective, a segment may be attractive because a firm has the resources and capabilities to deliver on the needs of those in the segment. From an external perspective, a segment may be attractive because it is profitable, has high growth potential, and/or is currently underserved. Targeting an attractive segment allows a firm to more effectively utilize its limited resources to focus on those areas of the market where it can be most successful.

Underlying Theory

The rationale for segmentation analysis is that to achieve competitive advantage and superior performance, firms should (1) identify segments of industry demand and unique abilities to serve particular segments, (2) target specific segments of demand that they are able to serve, and (3) develop specific strategies for each targeted market segment.[1] From an economic perspective, segmentation is built on the assumption that heterogeneity in demand and supply allows for demand to be disaggregated into segments with distinct demand functions and for a firm to leverage unique resources and capabilities in supplying a market segment.[2]

Segmentation analysis is therefore based on the concepts of *market* and *firm heterogeneity*—the idea that market participants have different wants and needs and that firm resources and capabilities are different from one firm to the next. *Market heterogeneity* is the notion not only that customers display differences in current and past characteristics but also that these differences are predictors of their future behavior.[3] Ignoring the effect of heterogeneity in markets might cause managers in firms to overlook specific customer needs and underserve sectors of a market.

The concept of *firm heterogeneity* has its theoretical roots in the resource-based view (RBV) of the firm, which views a firm as a bundle of *resources* and *capabilities*. Resources are defined as "those (tangible and intangible) assets which are tied semi-permanently to the firm."[4] *Capabilities* are organizational managerial skills used to orchestrate a diverse set of resources and deploy them in a way that creates value. Capabilities tend to be intangible, and they differ across firms. Firms have different strategic resources and capabilities, and resources and capabilities tend to be *sticky*, that is, not perfectly mobile across firms. Therefore, unique resources and capabilities are important antecedents for firm strategizing and performance.[5]

Segmentation analysis is a structured approach to match the unique needs of specific market participants with the specific resources and capabilities of a firm, in a way that creates value for both the firm and the market participants.

Core Idea

Segmentation analysis is commonly summed up in the S-T-P framework. In this framework the S stands for *segmentation*, the T stands for *targeting*, and the P stands for *positioning*. That is, a market is segmented, one or more segments are selected for targeting, and products or services are positioned as part of a firm's strategy in a way that resonates with the selected target market or markets.

The first phase is to identify the market and then to establish a basis for segmenting the market. To find a basis for segmentation, a market manager should look for a means of achieving internal homogeneity (similarity within the segments) and external heterogeneity (differences between segments). In other words, they are searching for a process that minimizes differences between members of a segment and maximizes differences between each segment. In addition, the segmentation approach must yield segments that are meaningful for the firm and its offering. For example, a person's eye color may be a relevant basis for a make-up manufacturer, but it would not be relevant for a seller of financial services. Selecting the right base requires a good deal of thought and a solid understanding of the market to be segmented. The ideal basis for market segmentation is identifiable, substantial, accessible, responsive, and actionable.[6]

- *Identifiable* refers to the extent to which managers can identify or recognize distinct groups within the marketplace.
- *Substantial* refers to the extent to which a segment or group of customers represents a sufficient size to be profitable. This could mean sufficiently large in number of people or in purchasing power.
- *Accessible* refers to the extent to which marketers can reach the targeted segments with promotional or distribution efforts.
- *Responsive* refers to the extent to which consumers in a defined segment are likely to respond to marketing offers targeted at them.
- *Actionable* refers to the degree to which segments provide guidance for marketing decisions.

Table 16.1 provides a description of many of the factors that typically serve as a base for identifying market segments.

After identifying the basis for segmentation and segmenting a market, the next key decision is which segment a firm should target. Evaluating potential segments to target typically involves

Table 16.1 Factors Used to Identify Market Segments

Segmentation Base	Brief Explanation of Base	Example Segments
Demographic	Quantifiable population characteristics (e.g., age, gender, income, education, socioeconomic status, family size or situation)	Young, upwardly mobile, prosperous professionals (yuppies); double income no lids (DINKS); graying, leisured, and moneyed (GLAMS); empty nester, full nester
Geographic	Physical location or region (e.g., country, state, region, city, suburb, postcode)	New Yorkers; remote, outback Australians; urbanites; inner-city dwellers
Geo-demographic (or geoclusters)	Combination of geographic and demographic variables	Rural farmers, urban professionals, "sea changers," "tree changers"
Psychographics	Lifestyle, social, or personality characteristics (typically includes basic demographic descriptors)	Socially aware; traditionalists; conservatives; active "club-going" young professionals
Behavioral	Purchasing, consumption, or usage behavior (e.g., needs based, benefit sought, usage occasion, purchase frequency, customer loyalty, buyer readiness)	Tech-savvy (aka tech-heads); heavy users, enthusiasts; early adopters; opinion leaders; luxury seekers; price conscious; quality conscious; time poor
Contextual and situational	The same consumer changes in their attractiveness to marketers based on context and situation. This is particularly used in digital targeting via programmatic bidding approaches	Actively shopping; just entering into a life change event; being physically in a certain location or at a particular retailer that is known from GPS data via smartphones

assessment of (1) segment size and growth, (2) segment structural attractiveness, and (3) firm objectives and resources. Some key questions to consider in assessing each of these elements can be found in Table 16.2.

When the target segments have been determined, the manager's next task is to design an approach that will resonate with, and deliver to, the target segments. This is commonly referred to as positioning.

Table 16.2 Key Questions to Consider in Assessing Market Segments

Segment Size and Growth	Segment Structural Attractiveness	Firm Objectives and Resources
• How large is the market? • Is the market segment substantial enough to be profitable? • Is the market segment growing or contracting? • What are the indications that growth will be sustained in the long term? Is any observed growth sustainable? • Is the segment stable over time?	• To what extent are competitors targeting this market segment? • Do buyers have bargaining power in the market? • Are substitute products available? • Can we carve out a viable position to differentiate from any competitors? • How responsive are members of the market segment to the marketing program? • Is this market segment reachable and accessible?	• Is this market segment aligned with our company's operating philosophy? • Do we have the resources necessary to enter this market segment? • Do we have prior experience with this market segment or similar market segments? • Do we have the skills and/or know-how to enter this market segment successfully?

This requires knowledge of target segments' needs, values, purchasing habits, and price sensitivity, among other things, and then developing and implementing offers and approaches that deliver value to the target segments. Positioning is often seen as a marketing tactic, but in successful firms the process of positioning is much broader and goes much deeper than marketing alone. It impacts a firm's operations, human resource processes, research and development, and finances. All these functions need to be aligned to deliver products and services that will meet the needs of the target segments.

Depiction

Figure 16.1 provides a visual depiction of the key elements of the segmentation analysis process, which include first segmenting the customer base, then targeting key segments, and finally positioning a firm's offering and strategic position to deliver to the targeted segment.

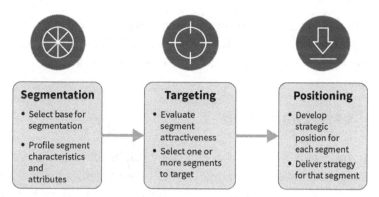

Figure 16.1. Segmentation tool for identifying, targeting, and positioning a product or service for a specific customer group.

Process

1. Identify market to be segmented.
2. Select basis for segmentation.
3. Profile segments' characteristics and attributes.
4. Evaluate segments' attractiveness.
5. Select one or more segments to target.
6. Develop strategic position for each segment.
7. Deliver strategy to position firm in targeted segments.

Insight or Value Created

Segmentation is a useful tool to help managers answer the important strategic questions of "where to play" and "how to win." Segmentation analysis helps managers think about which subsections of a market are most attractive and what to do to pursue those subsections. As such, it provides a structured way for firms to identify the most attractive customer groups to pursue and to structure their strategy to deliver value to those groups. It is a means to match market needs and wants with firm resources and capabilities.

Performing and implementing a high-quality segmentation analysis aids the firm to most effectively leverage its limited resources to create value for the market and, in so doing, create value for itself.

Risks and Limitations

In performing a segmentation analysis it can be difficult to manage the balance between becoming too niche (not having a big enough market to serve) and being too broad (not clearly identifying narrow enough segments to make the exercise meaningful). Some managers end up with segments that are too narrow and small, and others generate segments that are too broad and generic. In either case the process is less beneficial.

A second challenge associated with segmentation analysis is that segments are almost never static. They tend to change over time. Structural shifts, competitive dynamics, changing preferences, and technology disruptions may all cause segments to change, and when they do, firms may suddenly discover that their offerings are out of alignment with their target segments. Therefore, the S-T-P process needs to be continually monitored and re-evaluated to ensure that the firm remains strategically positioned to deliver value to its target segments.

Third, for some undifferentiated products, economies of scale and scope may render the mass market to be the most attractive segment. In those circumstances, any attempt to use segmentation analysis too rigorously might overlook the mass market opportunity that exists. Hence, managers should always carefully consider to what extent segmentation is meaningful in relation to the firm's products and capabilities.

Case Illustration: Harley-Davidson

Context

Let us return once more to Harley-Davidson to illustrate the use of segmentation analysis. As we mentioned, Harley-Davidson faced some significant challenges over the course of 2016 to 2018. Shipments fell, retail sales declined, and plants were closed. We previously already diagnosed Harley's predicaments through the lens of five-forces analysis (Chapter 7) and VRIO analysis (Chapter 9), in which we noted, among other things, the decreasing attractiveness of Harley's traditional focus on big, heavyweight motorcycles and the opportunity to exploit currently neglected resources and capabilities. Absent from this discussion thus far has been an in-depth segmentation of Harley-Davidson's customers. This is all the more relevant in this case, since Harley's traditional focus on heavyweight bikes mostly appealed to a quite specific customer segment: American middle-aged men with disposable income. As U.S. baby boomers got older—we noted that the average Harley rider's age has inched up to almost fifty[7]—Harley realized it would need to look at new products and segments to secure the future.[8]

Finding a New Customer Segment

As we mentioned, confronted with an aging customer base and younger, more price-sensitive individuals hesitant to embrace the iconic brand,[9] Harley set out to build a next generation of riders. Who should these riders be? This is where segmentation analysis can help.

Step 1: Identify market to be segmented. In this case, a broad approach to doing this for Harley-Davidson would be to think globally of adult men and women (as well as somewhat younger people who reach adulthood over the next three to seven years) who would be willing and able to buy and ride a motorcycle.

Step 2: Select basis for segmentation. For Harley-Davidson, the following segmentation parameters would seem make to make the most sense:

- *Age.* Given the current main segment's age, appealing to younger people was key.

- *Gender.* Given the current focus on men, attracting women was a great opportunity.
- *Income.* Riding a Harley is considered expendable, and hence only people above a certain income threshold were able to buy one.
- *Physical location.* The slumping sales in the United States were partially offset by international sales, and growth markets like Asia offered a huge opportunity.
- *Lifestyle.* What's consistent (and should probably remain consistent) is Harley's focus on selling more than just a product. That is, customers bought more than a motorcycle—they bought into a lifestyle.[10] People who are not amenable to this would constitute an unlikely segment.

Step 3: Profile the segments' characteristics and attributes. Based on these bases for segmentation, we can profile a few key segments that *might* be attractive. For the sake of illustration, let us focus on the following two possible segments:

- International (meaning non-U.S.) men aged twenty to fifty-five, with a two times average local income who are open to a rebel image and who value freedom
- U.S. women aged eighteen to forty, with a two times average income and who value freedom

Step 4: Evaluate the segments' attractiveness. In this step, we gauge the segments' attractiveness based on available data. Where no such data exist, companies need to go out and collect them. Talking to (potential) customers is key here (as Harley started doing, albeit rather late[11]). While we lack the kind of in-depth data needed to more thoroughly analyze these segments, at a high level, both would seem to be quite attractive, given the following:

- Both markets are large, and largely untapped by Harley at the time, and certainly substantial enough to be profitable.

- As for the U.S. younger women segment, according to the Motorcycle Industry Council, in the United States only 25% of all riders were age twenty-five to forty; just 14 % were women.[12]
- As for the international segment, European and Asian markets were experiencing growth. In Asia, people were turning to small, lightweight motorcycles to navigate crowded cities.[13] The Pew Research Center reported that 80% of households in Indonesia, Thailand, and Vietnam owned a motorcycle or scooter. Europe was also promising, with a large and growing market and preference for using a bike for commuting and for long-distance touring.[14] Harley's sales in Europe were already on the rise.
- Harley should be able to carve out a viable position to differentiate from competitors in these markets.
- However, competitors like Honda, Suzuki, Yamaha, Ducati, Kawasaki, and BMW were already actively pursuing these customers, and the traditional Harley product offering did not readily appeal to these segments. In addition, a critic might claim that Harley lacks experience with these segments. These would be two obvious hurdles to overcome.

Step 5: Select one or more segments to target. Since both segments seem to be reasonably attractive and match with firm objectives and resources, and since there is a clear strategic mandate to move away from the thus far dominant segment, let us conclude at a high level that both of these segments have potential.

Step 6: Develop a strategic position for each segment. This is what Harley-Davidson started actively pursuing. According to Harley's company strategy, by 2027 Harley would, among other things, (1) build two million new riders in the United States and (2) grow international business to over 50% of annual volume. Harley-Davidson's strategic positioning vis-à-vis the segments we outlined is focused on developing new motorcycles, including lighter-weight models and electric models of varying weights and sizes. New street bikes should also appeal to the identified segments. Besides new products, Harley also aims to broaden its access (online and through smaller, urban storefronts globally) to expose itself to these new customers.

Step 7: Deliver on the strategy to position the firm in the targeted segments. At the time of writing, Harley-Davidson was in the process of trying to deliver on its new strategy. Harley has developed its electric motorcycle, the LiveWire, to appeal to the targeted new segments, which will soon be followed by several other electric models. Two adventure touring bikes are expected to debut in 2020.[15] Another key element related to the global customer segment that we outlined earlier includes Harley starting to manufacture European bikes overseas, likely in preexisting Asian plants.[16]

In line with the objectives of segmentation analysis, the new Harley-Davidsons are intended to appeal to a new type of rider, based on a different industry positioning, while still capitalizing on Harley's VRIO resources. In the words of CEO Matthew Levatich: "We are turning a page in the history of the company. We're opening our arms to the next generation."[17]

17
Vertical Integration

Purpose and Objective

A key strategic decision for managers and practitioners is deciding on the scope of assets to be owned and controlled by a firm (i.e., what should be owned by a firm and what should be purchased or outsourced?). A vertical integration framework (sometimes also called a make-or-buy framework) provides a structured way to think about such decisions. It helps managers and practitioners make decisions about which assets and elements of a value chain a firm should own and which they can buy from other firms.

Vertical integration decisions have been a central element of strategy for many years. Famous vertical integration efforts include Henry Ford's decision to establish total control of the automobile manufacturing supply chain. By the 1920s his company ran coal and iron ore mines, timberlands, rubber plantations, a railroad, freighters, sawmills, blast furnaces, a glassworks, and more.

Underlying Theory

The theory underlying the vertical integration framework is that of transaction cost economics (TCE). In 2009 Oliver Williamson was awarded the Nobel Prize for developing the central ideas underpinning TCE. This is taken from the honoree statement associated with his Nobel Prize:[1]

> Transaction Cost Economics is a central theory in the field of Strategy. It addresses questions about why firms exist in the first place (i.e., to

minimize transaction costs), how firms define their boundaries, and how they ought to govern operations.

In Transaction Cost Economics, the starting point is the individual transaction (the synapse between the buyer and the seller). The question then becomes: Why are some transactions performed within firms rather than in the market, as the neoclassical view prescribes? The answer, not surprisingly, is because markets break down.

As a consequence of human cognitive limitations, coupled with the costs associated with transacting, the basic assumptions associated with efficient markets (e.g., anonymous actors, atomistic actors, rational actors, perfect information, homogeneous goods, the absence of liquidity constraints) fail to hold. For these reasons, it is often more advantageous to structure transactions within firms. And this is why firms are not just ubiquitous in our society, but also worthy of study in their own right. This contrasts with the typical view of firms in neoclassical economic theory as, at worst, a market aberration that ought not exist, and at best, a black box production function.

Williamson's contributions to the field of Transaction Cost Economics complement, and extend, those of Coase. First, Williamson started with an explicitly behavioral assumption of human behavior (bounded rationality). Second, he recognized that transacting parties sometimes behave opportunistically and take advantage of their counterparties. Finally, he identified features of transactions (e.g., specificity, uncertainty, frequency) that cause markets to fail, and hence, are likely to lead certain transactions to be organized within firms (hierarchies) rather than markets.

From Williamson's work on TCE, we recognize that the difficulty of writing a contract to manage a transaction is impacted by three key factors: specificity, uncertainty, and frequency. When these factors are present, it may be more beneficial to own an asset than to transact with others to get access to the asset via the market. These three factors are elaborated upon here:

- *Specificity of the assets* involved in the transaction. The more specific the assets involved in the transaction (i.e., they cannot be used or sold for other purposes), the greater the chance that one party in the transaction may "hold up" the contract to extract extra value; hence, writing a contract is more difficult and there is higher benefit for a firm in owning the asset (i.e., vertical integration).

- *Uncertainty* of the transaction. The higher the uncertainty associated with a transaction, the more difficult it is to write a contract allowing others to use or produce the asset, resource, or activity, and the higher the benefit of owning it (i.e., vertical integration).
- *Transaction frequency*. The higher the frequency of transactions associated with an asset, resource, or activity, the greater the chance of haggling over contracts every time firms transact, and hence the greater the benefit for a firm in owning the asset, resource, or activity (i.e., vertical integration).

Core Idea

Vertical integration considerations may take one of two broad forms: *forward integration* or *backward integration*. Forward integration entails a firm purchasing or creating a downstream operator in the supply chain (e.g., Apple opening its own chain of retail stores). Backward integration entails a firm purchasing or creating an upstream supplier (e.g., Starbucks acquiring coffee plantations in Costa Rica or Netflix getting into the development of original TV content).

Two dimensions are critical for a vertical integration decision. First, there is the question of "How easy or difficult is it to write contracts (for the transactions related to an asset, resource, or activity)?" The answer to this question is informed by the TCE factors of (1) specificity of the assets involved in the transaction, (2) uncertainty of the transaction, and (3) frequency of the transaction. Second, there is the dimension of "How critical is the management of the asset, resource, or activity to the creation and maintenance of competitive advantage?" An asset, resource, or activity should be owned if mismanagement has a big effect on the firm's competitive advantage.

The more difficult it is to write contracts pertaining to the management of an asset, the more necessary or valuable it may be to vertically integrate (i.e., own) that asset. The more critical the management of an asset (and related activities) is to the creation and maintenance of the competitive advantage of a firm, the more necessary and valuable it may be for the firm to *own* that asset (i.e., vertically integrate or avoid outsourcing). Hence, it is important to assess the relative importance of an asset to a firm's competitive advantage. To do this, managers and practitioners need to recognize the resources and capabilities that combine to create a competitive advantage for a firm and assume control of those resources and capabilities, even if it would be easy to write a contract to acquire such resources and capabilities.

Note that the framework indicates that even in situations where it may be very difficult to write effective contracts (e.g., high asset specificity), vertical de-integration may be optimal. Likewise, in situations where it may be easy to write contracts, the optimal choice may be vertical integration (see Figure 17.1).

Depiction

Figure 17.1 provides a visual depiction of the framework that can be used to inform vertical integration decisions by factoring in the importance of an activity for a firm's competitive advantage and the degree of difficulty to write contracts for that activity.[2]

Process

1. Lay out stages in an industry supply chain or business activity system and identify assets, resources, or activities associated with each stage.

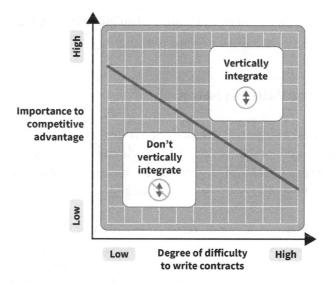

Figure 17.1. Vertical integration tool to inform "make or buy" decisions.

2. Identify participants at each stage; classify transactions across stages. Transactions may be once off, contractual, or internal transfers.

3. Assess the ease with which contracts can be written for each transaction. To do this consider (a) the frequency of transactions, (b) the uncertainty of transactions, and (c) the specificity of the asset. Higher frequency, greater uncertainty, and higher asset specificity make it more problematic to write contracts for each transaction.

4. Assess the extent to which different assets, resources, or activities create (or have the potential to create) a competitive advantage for a firm within a supply chain or business activity system.

5. Evaluate where the assets, resources, or activities within a supply chain or business activity system fall on the two-dimensional framework with (a) the degree of difficulty to write contracts on one axis and (b) the importance to competitive advantage on the other axis.

6. Use the framework in Figure 17.1 to guide the decision about what to integrate and what to buy or source.

Insight or Value Created

The vertical integration framework creates a systematic way for managers and practitioners to work through strategic decisions pertaining to firm scope. It gives them a means to evaluate carefully what a firm should own and what it might buy or source from the outside.

Many strategic decisions relate to firm scope. Over time, there have been waves of vertical integration and vertical de-integration as different management philosophies have come in vogue. Whatever the trend at the time, it is important to analyze such decisions carefully and systematically. The framework discussed here provides a means to do so.

Risks and Limitations

This framework depends on managers' and practitioners' ability to properly understand and categorize the assets, resources, or activities within a supply chain or business activity system. Doing so is difficult, and if managers or practitioners get it wrong (e.g., they overlook a key asset, resource, or activity or misclassify it), then the framework may lead to invalid decisions.

It can also be difficult to objectively evaluate the extent to which an asset, resource, or activity is central to competitive advantage and to assess how difficult it is to write a contract for a transaction. The judgments may vary depending on the experience and perspective of the person making the judgment; hence, the decisions stemming from this framework may depend on who is using it.

The framework tends to prompt strategic decisions based on current and historic data rather than on how things may play out in the future. In this sense, it provides something of a static analysis rather than dynamic insight. There are ways to incorporate a more dynamic perspective, but this can be complex, subjective, and difficult to do.[3]

Case Illustration: Starbucks

Context

Howard Schultz acquired Starbucks Coffee in 1987 for $3.8 million. At the time, the company owned just six retail stores in Seattle and was focused primarily on selling roasted coffee beans. They did not sell espresso or other coffee beverages. Schultz had been inspired by coffee bars in Milan, Italy, where locals go daily to buy an espresso; he wanted to use Starbucks as a foundation to focus on selling ready-to-drink coffee and espresso, and he wanted to scale the business across the United States. Schultz set the goal to "establish Starbucks as the premier purveyor of the finest coffee in the world while maintaining uncompromising principles as we grow." To deliver on this, he needed to decide what elements of the firm's value chain should be owned and controlled by Starbucks and what elements should be owned and controlled by others. In other words, Schultz needed to make careful vertical integration decisions to not only create a model that would allow Starbucks to deliver on its core value proposition of quality and customer experience but also be scalable across the United States and later abroad.

Analyzing Vertical Integration Decisions at Starbucks

Step 1: Lay out stages in an industry supply chain or business activity system and identify assets, resources, or activities associated with each stage. In the case of Starbucks, this entails laying out the industry supply chain for retailing coffee, including the assets, resources, and activities associated with each stage. Table 17.1 provides an overview of the coffee industry supply chain.

Table 17.1 Overview of the Coffee Industry Supply Chain

	Growing Coffee Beans	Processing Coffee Beans	Exporters	Roasting Coffee Beans	Packaging and Distribution	Retailing Coffee Beans	Retailing Brewed Coffee
Assets, resources, and activities	Farms, plantations	Wet mill, dry mill	Shipping companies	Coffee roasting plant	Packaging machinery, fleet of vehicles	Physical retail store, online retail store	Coffee shop, coffee machines

Step 2: Identify participants at each stage; classify transactions across stages. Transactions may be once off, contractual, or internal transfers. Table 17.2 identifies the assets, resources, and capabilities at each stage of the coffee supply chain, as well as the participants, and then classifies the transactions between participants.

Steps 3 and 4: Assess the ease with which contracts can be written for each transaction. To do this consider (a) the frequency of transactions, (b) the uncertainty of transactions, and (c) the specificity of the asset. Higher frequency, greater uncertainty, and higher asset specificity make it more problematic to write contracts for each transaction. Assess the extent to which different assets, resources, or activities create (or have the potential to create) competitive advantage for a firm within a supply chain or business activity system. Table 17.3 assesses the ease with which contracts can be written for each transaction in the coffee supply chain, as well as the importance of each transaction for a competitive advantage for Starbucks.

Steps 5 and 6: Evaluate where the assets, resources, or activities within a supply chain or business activity system fall on the two-dimensional framework with (a) degree of difficulty to write contracts on one axis and (b) importance to competitive advantage on the other axis. Use the framework in Figure 17.1 to guide the decision about what to integrate and what to buy or source. Table 17.4 provides an overview of Starbucks's vertical integration decisions in 1987.

Table 17.2 Coffee Supply Chain Transactions

	Growing Coffee Beans	Processing Coffee Beans	Exporters	Roasting Coffee Beans	Packaging and Distribution	Retailing Coffee Beans	Retailing Brewed Coffee
Assets, resources, and activities	Farms, plantations	Wet mill, dry mill	Shipping	Coffee roasting plant	Packaging machinery, fleet of vehicles	Physical retail store, online retail store	Coffee bar, coffee machines
Participants	Farmers	Mill owners	Exporters and shipping firms	Coffee roasters	Distributors	Retailers	Coffee bar owners
Transactions		A. In some cases coffee farmers form a co-op to own and manage their own mills, making this transaction an internal transfer; otherwise, the transaction is likely contractual.	B. Mill owners mostly supply exporters as a once-off transaction; processed coffee is typically sold in the open market.	C. Exporters supply to coffee roasters through contractual or once-off transactions.			

Continued

Table 17.2 Continued

Growing Coffee Beans	Processing Coffee Beans	Exporters	Roasting Coffee Beans	Packaging and Distribution	Retailing Coffee Beans	Retailing Brewed Coffee
				D. Some (many) coffee roasters do their own packaging and distribution; others contract this out or sell to packing and distribution firms		
					E. Some retailers package and distribute their coffee; others retail coffee packaged and distributed by others.	
						F. When Schultz first took over Starbucks, very few people retailed specialty brewed coffee.

Table 17.3 Vertical Integration Assessment of Starbucks

Transaction Parties	Ease of Writing Contracts for Transaction (Based on Frequency, Uncertainty, and Asset Specificity)	Importance of Transaction for Competitive Advantage for Starbucks	Vertical Integration Arrangement When Schultz Acquired Starbucks
A. Farmers— Mill owners	**Moderately difficult to contract**; this is why some farmers have cooperated to own mills	**Moderately high;** Starbucks depends on high-quality beans and effective milling to produce high-quality raw materials	Not integrated
B. Mill owners— Exporters	**Easy to contract;** open market for coffee, high-frequency and nonspecific assets	**Moderately low;** milling can make a difference, but export/import arrangements make no competitive difference	Not integrated
C. Exporters— Roasters	**Easy to contract;** open market for coffee, high-frequency and nonspecific assets	**Moderately low;** Starbucks does not depend on differentiated export/import arrangements for advantages	Not integrated
D. Roasters— Packers and distributors	**Moderately difficult to contract;** quality of roasted coffee can vary substantially, difficult to control	**High;** when Schultz took over, Starbucks advantage centered around its brand and quality of coffee, which links back to roasting and packaging	Integrated; Starbucks did all its own roasting and distribution to its own stores
E. Packers and distributors— Bean retailers	**Easy to contract;** high frequency of transactions and no asset specificity	**Moderate;** Starbucks could get others to package and distribute its product without impacting advantage	Integrated; Starbucks did all its own distribution to its own retail stores

Continued

Table 17.3 Continued

Transaction Parties	Ease of Writing Contracts for Transaction (Based on Frequency, Uncertainty, and Asset Specificity)	Importance of Transaction for Competitive Advantage for Starbucks	Vertical Integration Arrangement When Schultz Acquired Starbucks
F. Bean retailers— Coffee bars	Easy to contract	High; the Starbucks coffee shop experience is central to Starbucks's proposed competitive advantage, which centers on customer experience	Nonexistent; the concept of coffee bar selling specialty brewed coffee did not exist in the United States

Delivering on the Decision

Starbucks, under Schultz, made the clear and distinct decision not to franchise Starbucks stores in the United States; it owned all its own stores, thereby integrating the primary retail activities. This went counter to the growth strategy of many food retail outlets that adopted franchising as their primary growth strategy. As the Starbucks brand became known, the firm expanded its retail footprint to sell its coffee beans in other stores. It outsourced many aspects of the packaging and distribution process, allowing other firms with expertise in these areas to help it scale. Starbucks retained control of the roasting process and invested in larger roasting plants to facilitate growth. The firm consistently used outsourced shipping firms to import processed beans from abroad, yet it became intimately involved in sourcing beans from farmers and from coffee bean processing plants. As the firm grew, it even experimented with buying its own coffee plantations.[4] Although the firm would never be able to own all the coffee plantations from where it sourced raw material, owning some of the coffee plantations allowed it to *learn, experiment, and innovate.* Starbucks CEO Howard Schultz explained,

Table 17.4 Overview of Starbucks's Vertical Integration Decisions in 1987

	Growing Coffee Beans	Processing Coffee Beans	Exporters	Roasting Coffee Beans	Packaging and Distribution	Retailing Coffee Beans	Retailing Brewed Coffee
Assets, resources, and activities	Farms, plantations	Wet mill, dry mill	Shipping companies	Coffee roasting plant	Packaging machinery, fleet of vehicles	Physical retail store, online retail store	Coffee shop, coffee machines
Integration decision in 1987	Possibly integrate, easy to not that easy to contract and has impact on quality of coffee	Possibly integrate, easy to not that easy to contract and has impact on quality of coffee	Don't integrate, easy to contract and no impact on competitive advantage	Already integrated, *remain integrated* to retain control over roasting process	Already integrated, *but not necessary to keep integrated,* could look for outsourced packaging and distribution partners	Already integrated, *remain integrated but for now* could also look for other retail partners over time	Important to integrate to control the customer experience

"We are talking about doing innovative things we would not be able to do without this farm." Craig Russell, a Starbucks senior vice president, explained that the company would try to identify ways to address a fungus problem that was affecting coffee farm yields in Central America: "It's a dynamic situation and we will absolutely use this farm for testing different methodologies and ways to use new types of coffee trees we've developed that have become more disease- and rust-resistant." Finally, and most important, Starbucks intends to share what it learns about the fungus with other farmers, so that coffee bean production improves overall for the industry.[5]

18

Market Entry Modes

Purpose and Objective

The purpose behind this framework is to provide insight into the options that a firm has when it wishes to expand into a new market. Many (if not most) strategies seek to generate revenue growth, and much of the time that growth is sought in new markets. Seeking revenue growth from new markets may include pursuing the following:

- New geographic markets (e.g., selling in a new country or region)
- New product markets (e.g., applying a firm's insight or technology to develop a new type of product)
- New customer segments (e.g., seeking to sell to a different category of customers)
- A combination of the previous entries

When doing any of these, a firm has an array of options available with respect to how it may enter a new market. These may include direct exports, licensing, alliances, joint ventures, acquisitions, or setting up greenfield operations to name a few. Managers and practitioners need to understand the options available and the pros and cons of each option to make the right strategic decision about how to enter a new market.

Underlying Theory

The basic theory underlying the market entry mode framework suggests that there is a natural trade-off between control and cost when selecting a mode to enter a new market. Different entry modes imply a different level of control—meaning authority over operational and strategic decision-making—within an expanded operation. Different entry modes also require different resource commitments, meaning dedicated assets that cannot be redeployed for alternative uses without significant loss of value. These may be tangible (e.g., physical plant) or intangible (e.g., management know-how). In addition to cost and control considerations, a firm should also consider dissemination risk, which refers to the risk that specialized know-how will be expropriated by another entity (e.g., a licensing or joint venture partner).

This theory was initially developed primarily to account for a firm's options when expanding internationally, but it applies equally to decisions about entering new product or customer markets. As a firm seeks to have greater control over its expanded operations, the cost of expansion tends to increase.[1] The risk of losing know-how tends to be greater with options over which a firm has lower control. But this is not a pure either-or trade-off between cost and control. The strategic intention of market expansion should also factor into this decision. Some firms may be pursuing a centralized strategy where they are trying to standardize things across different areas of the business, and in such cases will likely prefer high-control entry modes, whereas other firms may be much more decentralized with localized units, and in such cases low-control entry modes may better align with their broader objectives.[2]

Core Idea

The core elements of the market entry mode framework are best reflected in a table. Table 18.1 highlights the various options in the leftmost column, with an indication of the level of investment, level of control, governance mechanisms, and pros and cons of each option in the other columns. This creates a summary of organizational arrangements that might be used to penetrate a new market that can help managers and practitioners make more informed choices and

Table 18.1 Market Entry Options

Option	Description	Cost	Control	Governance Mechanism	Pros	Cons
Direct exports	Taking orders in home market and shipping them direct to customers in a new market	Very low	Moderate	Governed through home market office	• Easy to initiate • No shared control or ownership	• High shipping times, costs, and complexity for individual items • Lack of sales and marketing presence in new market • No local adaptation
*Exporting via local distributor**	Entering an agreement for a local distributor to sell goods produced in home market in a new market	Low	Low	*Agency agreement* with agent in new market	• Flexible • Fast • Some local adaptation	• Limited financial return (captured by distributor) • Lack of control of sales process and customer experience
*Licensing**	Entering an agreement for local manufacturer to produce and sell goods in a new market	Low	Low	*Formal contract* with licensee	• Flexible • Fast • Some local adaptation	• Limited financial return (captured by licensee) • Lack of control of manufacturing, sales process, and customer experience
Sales operation	Setting up a sales team in a new market to sell goods produced in home market	Moderate	Moderate	*Ownership* of sales operation in new market	• Limited investment • Learning about new market	• Difficult to establish relationships • Initial lack of understanding about market

Continued

Table 18.1 Continued

Option	Description	Cost	Control	Governance Mechanism	Pros	Cons
Equity investment[†]	Purchase minority stake in an existing firm in a new market, enter an agreement to work with the firm in that market	Moderate to high	Low to moderate	*Minority* ownership stake in *existing* entity	• Can develop trust • Can learn about market from partner	• Expensive to buy equity • Lack of control over partner's actions • Requires careful negotiation to establish relationship
Joint venture[†]	Creation of a new entity in a new market with one or more other firms as joint owners in the new entity	High	Moderate	*Shared* stake in *new* entity created by two or more parent firms	• Strong tie with partner • Opportunity to learn about market or technology from joint venture partner • Leverage partner's relationships	• Complex to set up—long negotiations • Significant investment • May be difficult to manage and make decisions over time
Acquisition	Purchasing a majority stake in an existing firm operating in a new market	Very high	High	*Majority* ownership stake in *existing* entity	• Leverage existing business processes, people, and relationships	• Expensive • Integration challenges • Management challenges over time
Greenfield	Setting up a new operation from scratch in a new market	Very high	High	*Full* ownership of newly created entity	• Full control of new operation • Replicate best practice from other areas of business	• High cost • Difficulty operating in new market with limited relationships and knowledge

* These types of arrangements are typically classified as *nonequity* strategic alliance.

[†] These types of arrangements are typically classified as *equity* strategic alliance.

decisions when formulating a strategy that involves entry into a new market.

Depiction

The different market entry modes are summarized in Figure 18.1 with investment required on one axis and degree of control on the other axis.

Process

1. Assess a firm's need for control in the new market. Does the firm need/desire total control in the new market, or is there a willingness to forgo control to minimize costs and/or maximize learning?

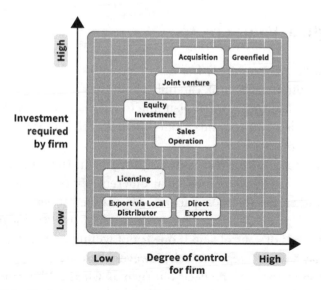

Figure 18.1. Market entry modes tool for comparing and contrasting different ways to enter a new market.

2. Assess the firm's willingness to invest in the new market. Is it willing to spend to establish a foothold in the market, or is there a preference to minimize investment and treat new market entry as more of an experiment?

3. Assess the firm's successes and failures in previous market entry attempts. Identify what can be learned from previous attempts to enter new markets.

4. Use the responses from the previous steps to narrow down the options for the firm. Once two or three options have been identified, do more research on each option:

   a. What rules or regulations might apply to each option?

   b. What alternatives are available under each option (e.g., distributor partners, licensing arrangements, investment options, strategic alliance partners, acquisition targets, etc.)?

   c. What other factors may impact each option?

5. Using the insight generated from the initial analysis and the more detailed analysis, debate the pros and cons of each option and use this to inform your strategic choice.

Insight or Value Created

The market entry options framework provides a way for managers and practitioners to think carefully about the array of options they have at their disposal when planning to enter a new market. It can also provide a way to think about different avenues for growth in a particular market.

Firms need to consider issues of investment (how much it will cost) and control when looking at different options for entering a new market. For the most part there is a trade-off between investment and control—it costs more in terms of investment to have higher levels of control, and if one is not willing to invest, then the firm may have to forego control. However, there are other issues that may also factor into the decision, such as whether the firm needs to learn about a new market, whether high levels of local adaption are required, and whether regulations necessitate a local partner. The framework provided here establishes an initial starting point for considering the options available and can be used to initiate more detailed research and analysis on a few alternatives.

Risks and Limitations

One of the challenges that arises when using the market entry framework is that successfully selecting an appropriate option for entering a new market is very context dependent, and the framework does not really account for the nuances of each context. Every situation is unique and needs to be assessed based on specific and diverse factors, yet the framework is unable to adequately account for all those factors.

A major factor determining the success of a market entry option is implementation and execution. Whichever option is chosen, it needs to be effectively implemented and executed to have any chance of success, yet the framework presented here does not account for execution effectiveness. For example, if managers decide to acquire a foreign subsidiary to enter an international market, a major factor impacting the success of that decision will be how firm managers integrate that acquisition. Hence, even if the right conceptual choice is chosen, that choice may fail because of poor delivery.

Case Illustration: Starbucks

Context

Soon after Howard Schultz acquired Starbucks, he set the goal to "establish Starbucks as the premier purveyor of the finest coffee in the world while maintaining uncompromising principles as we grow." According to Schultz, "We're not just selling a cup of coffee; we are providing an experience." To create coffee enthusiasts with deep dedication, Starbucks aims to provide exceptional-quality coffee and a seductive atmosphere in which to imbibe. Having begun to scale up Starbucks in 1985, by the mid- to late 1990s, analysts observed that the U.S. coffee-bar market appeared to be reaching saturation and the Starbucks store base was maturing, leading to a slowdown in the growth of unit volume and firm profitability. In response, Starbucks turned its attention to foreign markets for continued growth.

Seeking Opportunities in International Markets

In 1995, the firm established a subsidiary called Starbucks Coffee International Inc. as a means to push into international markets. Having identified potential markets in Asia, Europe, and South America, the managers at Starbucks Coffee International Inc. needed to decide *how* they would enter international markets. The market entry modes tool could help Starbucks Coffee International Inc. managers to assess which market entry options might be appropriate for their given situation. It lays out the various options and the key considerations associated with each option.

Step 1. Assess a firm's need for control in the new market. Does the firm need/desire total control in the new market, or is there a willingness to forgo control to minimize costs and/or maximize learning? The first step is for Starbucks managers to decide how much control they wish to exert over their operations in a new market. In the case of Starbucks, they initiated their international expansion with an overarching strategy focused on "customer experience." To nurture a meaningful experience, they needed insight into the culture of their target countries. In addition to this, they were targeting countries that are quite different in coffee-drinking habits, economic profile, and social norms compared to their home ground in North America.

Because of the importance of the customer experience and the brand to the Starbucks overall value proposition, the need for control of operations in a new market was relatively high. They also had a deep need to get access to premier retail locations in target countries.

Step 2. Assess the firm's willingness to invest in the new market. Are they willing to spend to establish a foothold in the market, or is there a preference to minimize investment and treat new market entry as more of an experiment? To do this, the Starbucks Coffee International Inc. managers would need to assess the willingness of the parent corporation to spend on the expansion; they would need to understand the investment parameters. This would entail strategic discussions within the organization about whether to start small and cheap, just to learn, or to make a more substantive investment to have an impact. Having an impact and delivering a good customer experience were important; hence, Starbucks decided it needed to be willing to invest more heavily.

Step 3. Assess the firm's successes and failures in previous market entry attempts. Identify what can be learned from previous attempts to enter new markets. In the early stages of expanding abroad at Starbucks, managers had no prior attempts at international expansion to learn from; in later attempts at market entry, they had many experiences to draw from and these had a big impact on their choices.

Step 4. Use the responses from the previous steps to narrow down the options for the firm. Once two or three options have been identified, do more research on each option. In the case of Starbucks, their need for control of the brand and the customer experience, along with the willingness to invest quite heavily in new countries, meant that the most reasonable options would be a greenfield, acquisition, or joint venture. Given the strong focus of Starbucks on its brand, it is unlikely that acquiring an existing coffee chain in a target market was an immediately attractive option. It would not be worth their while to pay for a firm with another brand and change it to the Starbucks brand. For the same reason, they likely eliminated the equity investment option. This leaves the greenfield and joint venture options as viable alternatives. Greenfield would give them total control but would also cut them off from access to existing local relationships and to insights about culture that could come from a local joint venture partner.

Knowing this, the Starbucks managers would investigate the regulations around foreign ownership in target countries for a greenfield operation and what the options might be for joint venture partners; they would also assess what other factors might impact each option.

Step 5. Using the insight generated from the initial analysis and the more detailed analysis, debate the pros and cons of each option and use this to inform your strategic choice. Armed with the necessary information, the Starbucks managers could vigorously debate the various options and even begin negotiations with potential joint venture partners or acquisition targets. Then, using this information, they would make their final strategic choice.

This prompted Starbucks to create an international market entry focused on joint ventures with local partners in target counties. *US News and World Report* described the approach they formulated as follows:

> When venturing overseas, there is a Starbucks way. The company finds local business partners in most foreign markets. . . . It tests each country with a handful of stores in trendy districts, using experienced Starbucks managers. It sends local baristas to Seattle for 13 weeks of training. Then it starts opening stores by the dozen. Its coffee lineup doesn't vary, but Starbucks does adapt its food to local tastes. In Britain, it won an award for its mince pie. In Asia, Starbucks offers curry puffs and meat buns. The company also fits its interior décor to the local architecture, especially in historic buildings. "We don't stamp these things out cookie-cutter style," says Peter Maslen, president of Starbucks Coffee International.[3]

Delivering on the Decision

Although Starbucks is committed to owning its North American stores, it has sought partners for much of its overseas expansion. As Kathy Lindemann, senior vice president of operations for Starbucks International, describes it:

Our approach to international expansion is to focus on the *partnership first, country second*. We rely on the local connection to get everything up and working. The key is finding the right local partners to negotiate local regulations and other issues. We look for partners who share our values, culture, and goals about community development. We are primarily interested in partners who can guide us through the process of starting up in a foreign location. We look for firms with: (1) similar philosophy to ours in terms of shared values, corporate citizenship, and commitment to be in the business for the long haul, (2) multi-unit restaurant experience, (3) financial resources to expand the Starbucks concept rapidly to prevent imitators, (4) strong real-estate experience with knowledge about how to pick prime real estate locations, (5) knowledge of the retail market, and (6) the availability of the people to commit to our project.

In an international joint venture, it is the partner that chooses store sites. These are submitted for approval to Starbucks, but the partner does all the preparatory and selection work.[4]

The first Starbucks location outside North America opened in Tokyo, Japan, in 1996 through a joint venture partnership with Sazaby Inc., which operates upscale retail and restaurant chains in Japan. A year later the Philippines became the nest Starbucks market outside North America through a partnership with Rustan's Corporation.

Then they changed tack and entered the U.K. market in 1998 with the $83 million acquisition of the then fifty-six-outlet, U.K.-based Seattle Coffee Company, rebranding all the stores as Starbucks.

19
Business Model Canvas

Purpose and Objective

The purpose of a business model canvas is to assess how the firm's economic activity is configured to create and deliver on a firm's value proposition. The business model canvas provides a holistic perspective of how the major elements of a business need to be aligned to allow the firm to create and capture value.

Managers and practitioners can use a business model canvas when first developing a business model for a new business or when revising or implementing a new strategy to assess how different elements of the business need to change to deliver on the new strategy.

Underlying Theory

The theoretical approach underlying the business model canvas is that of *design science*.[1] Buckminster Fuller, an architect, engineer, mathematician, poet, cosmologist, and forerunner of design science, described its essence as follows:

> The function of what I call design science is to solve problems by introducing into the environment new artifacts, the availability of which will induce their spontaneous employment by humans and thus, coincidentally, cause humans to abandon their previous problem-producing behaviors and devices. For example, when humans have a vital need to cross the roaring rapids of a river, as a design scientist I would design them a bridge, causing them, I am sure, to abandon

spontaneously and forever the risking of their lives by trying to swim to the other shore.[2]

March and Smith defined designed science as an attempt to create things that serve human purposes.[3] Osterwalder applied design science to design a business model framework that helps managers express the business logic of a firm in a new way, abandoning the former informal business logic descriptions.[4]

Influenced by the balanced scorecard approach[5] and more generally business management literature,[6] Osterwalder developed a framework emphasizing four key areas that a business model has to address:

- *Product*: what business the company is in, the products and the value propositions offered to the market
- *Customer interface*: who the company's target customers are, how it delivers customers products and services, and how it builds strong relationships with them
- *Infrastructure management*: how the company efficiently performs infrastructural or logistical issues, with whom, and as what kind of network enterprise
- *Financial aspects*: the revenue model, the cost structure, and the business model's sustainability

Core Idea

A business model describes the rationale of how an organization creates, delivers, and captures value.

The business model canvas is a strategic management template for documenting a firm's business model to visualize how the different elements of the business align to create and capture value. It is a visual chart with elements describing a firm's value proposition, infrastructure, customers, and finances. The different elements of a business model are accounted for in Table 19.1.

Table 19.1 Different Elements of a Business Model

Business Model Element	Description
Value proposition	The collection of products and services a business offers to meet the needs of its customers. A firm's value proposition is what distinguishes it from its competitors. The value proposition provides value through various elements such as newness, performance, customization, "getting the job done," design, brand, status, price, cost reduction, risk reduction, accessibility, convenience, and usability.
Customer segments	Identification of the customers that a firm intends to serve. Various sets of customers can be segmented based on the different needs and attributes. Doing so helps ensure appropriate implementation of a strategy that meets the characteristics of a selected group of clients. Some of the different types of generic customer segments include: • *Mass market:* There is no specific segmentation for a company that follows the mass market element as the organization displays a wide view of potential clients. • *Niche market:* Customer segmentation is based on specialized needs and characteristics of its clients. • *Segmented:* A company applies additional segmentation within the existing customer segment. In the segmented situation, the business may further distinguish its clients based on gender, age, and/or income. • *Diverse*: A business serves multiple customer segments with different needs and characteristics. • *Multisided Platform*: Serving two mutually dependent customer segments by creating a platform to connect them in a way that they provide value to one another; for example, a credit card company will provide services to credit card holders while also assisting merchants who accept those credit cards.
Channels	Channels reflect the mechanisms a firm uses to get its products or services to customers. Effective channels will distribute a company's value proposition in ways that are fast, efficient, and cost effective. An organization can reach its customers through its own channels (store front), partner channels (major distributors), or a combination of both.

Table 19.1 Continued

Business Model Element	Description
Customer relationships	Firms should identify the type of relationship they want to create with their customer segments. Various forms of customer relationships include: • *Personal assistance*: This is assistance in the form of employee–customer interaction. Such assistance is performed either during sales, after sales, or both. • *Self-service:* This is the type of relationship that translates from the indirect interaction between the company and the clients. Here, an organization provides the tools needed for the customers to serve themselves easily and effectively. • *Automated services:* This is a system similar to self-service but more personalized as it has the ability to identify individual customers and their preferences. An example of this would be Amazon.com making book suggestions based on the characteristics of the previous book purchased. • *Communities:* Creating a community allows for a direct interaction among different customers and the firm. The community platform produces a scenario where knowledge can be shared and problems are solved between different customers. • *Cocreation*: A personal relationship is created through the customer's direct input in the final outcome of the company's products/services.
Key resources	Key resources are the resources that are needed to create value for the customer. These are things the firm needs to own, lease, license, or hire to be able to create and deliver its value proposition. These resources could be human, financial, physical, or intellectual.
Key activities	These are the most important activities that a firm must engage in to create and deliver its value proposition. This accounts for the things that the firm must *do* to provide its value proposition.
Key partners	Key partners are the relationships that a firm fosters to be able to create and deliver its value proposition. Partnerships allow the firm to optimize operations and reduce risks. They enable a firm to focus on its core activity. Key partners may include suppliers, alliance partners, joint venture partners, and other firms or individuals on whom a firm depends to create and deliver its value proposition.

Continued

Table 19.1 Continued

Business Model Element	Description
Revenue streams	This is the way a firm makes income from each customer segment. Revenue streams may include the following: • *Asset sale*—selling ownership rights to a physical good • *Usage fee*—generating revenue by allowing the use of a particular service • *Subscription fees*—revenue generated by selling a continuous service • *Lending/leasing/renting*—giving exclusive right to an asset for a particular period of time • *Licensing*—revenue generated from charging for the use of a protected intellectual property • *Brokerage fees*—revenue generated from an intermediate service between two parties • *Advertising*—revenue generated from charging fees for product advertising
Cost structure	This describes most of the costs incurred to deliver, own, and manage the activities, resources, and partnerships needed to provide a firm's value proposition. Costs may be classified as follows: • *Fixed costs*—costs are unchanged across different applications. • *Variable costs*—these costs vary depending on the amount of production of goods or services. Costs may also be influenced by: • *Economies of scale*—costs go down as the amount of goods ordered or produced increases. • *Economies of scope*—costs go down due to incorporating other businesses, products, or services that are related to the original product.

Depiction

The business model elements are reflected on the business model canvas in nine interrelated boxes as depicted in Figure 19.1.[7]

Process

1. Develop and describe the firm's value proposition.

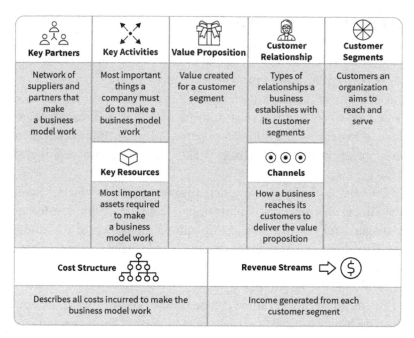

Figure 19.1. Business model canvas tool for describing the different elements of a firm's business model.

2. Identify and describe the customer segments to be served with the value proposition of the firm.
3. Identify and describe the channels and customer relationship mechanisms for reaching and working with customers.
4. Identify and describe the key resources, key activities, and key partnerships required to create and deliver the value proposition.
5. Identify and describe the different revenue streams from the focal customer segments.
6. Identify and describe the different costs incurred to provide the resources, activities, and partnerships to create and deliver the value proposition.
7. Map all of these on a business model canvas and evaluate whether they fit together; make changes as necessary.

Insight or Value Created

The business model canvas is partly a strategy formulation tool (developing the value proposition and aligning it with customer segments) and partly a strategy execution and delivery tool (assessing what channels, relationships, activities, and resources are needed to deliver on a value proposition). This interaction between strategy formulation and delivery makes for a useful and meaningful strategic discussion.

The value of the business model canvas comes from collecting and visualizing all aspects of the business in a single diagram. It forces managers and practitioners to think about all aspects of a business together. It creates a platform for them to debate and clarify how component parts of the business fit together and whether they make sense alongside one another.

The business model canvas can be used to assess whether a firm's existing business model can deliver on a chosen strategy and/or to develop a new business model to align with recent strategic choices, so as to deliver on those strategic choices.

Risks and Limitations

Although the business model canvas is one of the most useful and influential management and strategy tools developed in the last ten years, it does have some weaknesses and shortcomings.

First, users have recognized that learning to use the tool effectively can take time. The use of the tool is not always trivial and intuitive, and people tend to need practice to identify what to write in different boxes of the canvas.

Second, there are few specified relationships between the nine components of the tool. This makes it very difficult to show how a revenue stream is connected to a customer segment or how a key resource is driving up costs. Although these relationships can be inferred, it may not be obvious if they are out of alignment.

Third, it does not work very well as a communication tool. Once completed, most business model canvases are a cluttered and dense collection of ideas that are often difficult to read and challenging to synthesize into a coherent and clear overall picture.

Case Illustration: Spotify

Context

Spotify is a music streaming service that was founded in 2006 by Daniel Ek and Martin Lorentzon. It allows users to stream music, videos, and podcasts online through their website or through their software application. When the service first launched in 2008, it launched primarily as a paid service, with free accounts only available by invitation. This was done to manage growth and generate some income from the majority of users. At this time Spotify also had a limited portfolio of music. In its first year, the popularity of the service was very limited and thus organizational performance was poor; they needed to adjust their approach to find a more sustainable path to growth.

Business Model Analysis

In this situation, the business model canvas can help leaders, such as Ek and Lorentzon, conceptualize what could change to help their business to ignite grow and to understand how such changes might fit with everything else they do.

Step 1: Develop and describe the firm's value proposition. In this first step, the leaders of an organization will articulate the firm's intended value proposition for customers. In the case of Spotify, their initial value proposition could be framed as providing users with access to an array of music with personalization and recommendation based on individual users' music preferences. This would be captured in the center Value Proposition box of the business model canvas.

Step 2: Identify and describe the customer segments to be served with the value proposition of the firm. In this second step, leaders establish which customer segments they will serve. Spotify's initial focal customer segment was music lovers willing to pay for access to music; they focused heavily on invited users. This would be captured in the extreme left Customer Segment box of the business model canvas.

Step 3: Identify and describe the channels and customer relationship mechanisms for reaching and working with customers. In the third step, leaders establish the channels that will be used to get the value proposition to the customer and how customer relationships are forged and maintained. Spotify was designed as an online service, and hence it used Spotify.com as its channel; relationships were forged through online, self-service mechanisms through which the firm's computers would learn customers' preferences and personalize music for them. These insights are captured in the Channel and Customer Relationship boxes of the business model canvas.

Step 4: Identify and describe the key resources, key activities, and key partnerships required to create and deliver the value proposition. Having conceptualized the front end of the business, the next step is to establish what happens on the back end. For Spotify, this means identifying what resources they utilize, which include talented employees, algorithms for managing data, and contracts with record labels. The key activities include software development, music library management, and user acquisition via marketing. The key partners for Spotify are record labels and cloud computing service providers.

Step 5: Identify and describe the different revenue streams from the focal customer segments. Having established the basic elements of the operations of the business, it is important to understand the finances. This begins with identifying the key revenue streams. For Spotify, in the first iteration of their business model, revenue would come from user subscription fees. This is captured in the bottom right corner of the business model canvas.

Step 6: Identify and describe the different costs incurred to provide the resources, activities, and partnerships to create and deliver the value proposition. The costs for Spotify can be identified by understanding what the firm needs to pay for key resources and activities. In this case it includes royalties on music streamed, cloud storage expenses, salaries, and marketing expenses. These are captured in the bottom left corner of the business model canvas.

Step 7: Map all of these on a business model canvas and evaluate whether they fit together; make changes as necessary. With the business model canvas populated, one can see what the different elements of the business are and how they fit together. The business model canvas in Figure 19.2 illustrates what this would look like.

Using this initial depiction of the business model canvas, the Spotify team can see that Spotify was initially focused on a fairly restrictive market and not fully leveraging advertising opportunities. To explore options to increase growth, the team could manipulate key elements of the initial business model to examine how they may fit within the broader business. This might entail expanding the

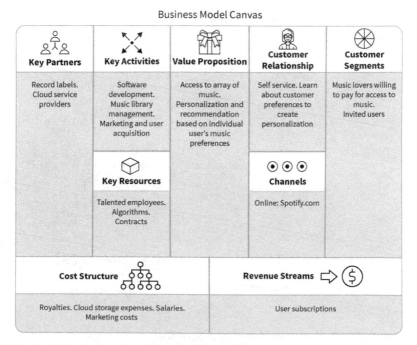

Figure 19.2. Business model canvas for Spotify when it first launched.

customer segments to appeal to a broader market, as well as building out the capability to sell and deliver advertising, which would generate an important additional source of revenue to supplement the expense of serving free users, as depicted in Figure 19.3.

The revised business model in Figure 19.3 illustrates how, in making this change, the Spotify team needs to manage different kinds of customers (users and advertisers) and how they need to create a value proposition, relationships, and channels for each. It also highlights that this may allow them to generate additional revenue and create more "free" accounts, thereby attracting many more users.

This is the essence of what Spotify did to grow their user base to the point where they had 159 million free users and 71 million paid subscribers at the time they became a public company in 2018.

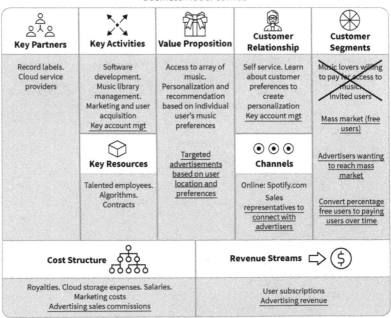

Figure 19.3. Business model canvas for Spotify after revising its business model.

20
Balanced Scorecard

Purpose and Objective

The purpose of the balanced scorecard is to provide a holistic perspective to setting firm goals and monitoring performance. Traditionally firms have focused on financial measures as an assessment of firm success, but financial outcomes are driven by a variety of other fundamental factors within a firm. The balanced scorecard prompts managers to set goals and measure performance for some of those other factors, including customers' views of the firm, internal business processes, and learning and growth among employees. The balanced scorecard therefore provides a financial, marketing, operations, and human resources perspective of a firm's performance.

When used to implement strategy, the balanced scorecard approach prompts managers and practitioners to think about what needs to happen in different elements of the business for the strategy to take hold. It encourages managers and practitioners to think about how the strategy will impact the customer, operational, and people processes to ultimately affect financial results.

Underlying Theory

The balanced scorecard draws on the concept of *management by objectives* introduced by Peter Drucker in his classic 1954 book, *The Practice of Management*. Drucker argued that all employees should have personal performance objectives that aligned strongly to the company strategy:

Each manager, from the "big boss" down to the production foreman or the chief clerk, needs clearly spelled-out objectives. These objectives should lay out what performance the man's own managerial unit is supposed to produce. They should lay out what contribution he and his unit are expected to make to help other units obtain their objectives. . . . These objectives should always derive from the goals of the business enterprise. . . . [M]anagers must understand that business results depend on a balance of efforts and results in a number of areas. . . . Every manager should responsibly participate in the development of the objectives of the higher unit of which his is a part. . . . He must know and understand the ultimate business goals, what is expected of him and why, what he will be measured against and how.[1]

Kaplan and Norton integrated the management-by-objectives concept with a number of other concepts to develop the balanced scorecard as a bridge across multiple literatures that had been created in complete isolation from each other: the literature on quality and lean management, which emphasizes employees' continuous improvement activities to reduce waste and increase company responsiveness; the literature on financial economics, which places heightened emphasis on financial performance measures; and stakeholder theory, in which a firm is viewed as an intermediary attempting to forge contracts that satisfy all its different constituents.[2] Kaplan and Norton attempted to retain the valuable insights from each:

- Employee and process performance are critical for current and future success.
- Financial metrics ultimately increase if a firm's performance improves.
- To optimize long-term shareholder value, a firm has to internalize the preferences and expectations of its shareholders, customers, suppliers, employees, and communities.

The key was to develop a more robust measurement and management system that included operational metrics as leading indicators and financial metrics as lagging outcomes, along with several other metrics to measure a company's progress in driving future performance.[3]

Core Idea

The core idea behind the balanced scorecard is to take a firm's strategy and translate it into goals, objectives, measures, targets, and initiatives in each of the four core areas of a firm: customers, processes, people, and finances. The firm is then managed according to the goals, objectives, measures, targets, and initiatives within each of the four core elements of the business. Strategy is thus implemented in a balanced way such that different internal and external processes within a business can support and reinforce each other. The core idea is to get operational, customer, people, and financial processes working together toward a common strategy.

Table 20.1 captures the core issues and focuses of each of the four perspectives within the balanced scorecard model.

Depiction

Figure 20.1 illustrates how the different balanced scorecard elements fit together and what needs to be specified in each.[4]

Process

1. Articulate the vision and strategy of the firm.
2. Transform the vision and strategy of the firm into objectives for each element of the scorecard—learning and growth, internal business processes, customers, and finances.
3. Specify the measures, targets, and initiatives for each of the objectives under each perspective in the balanced scorecard.

Table 20.1 Four Perspectives Within the Balanced Scorecard Model

Perspective	Focus
Financial	The financial performance elements of the balanced scorecard define the long-run financial objectives of a firm. While most businesses will emphasize profitability, other financial objectives are also possible, such as revenue growth or cash generation. Relevant financial measures may be related to a firm's lifecycle stage.
Customer	In the customer perspective of the balanced scorecard, managers identify the customer and market segments in which the business unit will compete and the measures of the firm's performance in these targeted segments. The customer perspective typically includes several generic measures of a successfully implemented strategy such as customer satisfaction, customer retention, new customer acquisition, customer profitability, and market and account share in targeted segments. While these measures may be somewhat generic, they should be customized to the targeted customer groups from whom the business unit expects its greatest growth and profitability to be derived.
Internal business processes	Under the internal business process perspective, executives identify the critical internal processes in which the firm must excel. The critical internal business processes enable the business unit to deliver on the value propositions for customers in targeted market segments and satisfy shareholder expectations of excellent financial returns. The measures should be focused on the internal processes that will have the greatest impact on customer satisfaction and achieving the organization's financial objectives.
Learning and growth	The learning and growth perspective identifies the requirements to be fulfilled to create long-term growth and improvement. Businesses are unlikely to be able to meet their long-term targets for customers and internal processes using today's technologies and capabilities. Also, intense global competition requires that companies continually improve their capabilities for delivering value to customers and shareholders.

This should translate into fifteen to twenty objectives, measures, targets, and initiatives within a firm.

4. Monitor performance of each initiative according to the targets, measures, and objectives that have been set.

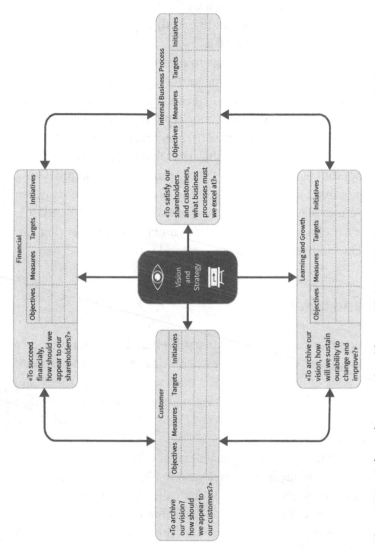

Figure 20.1. Balanced scorecard tool for establishing objectives, measures, targets, and initiatives across all aspects of a firm when delivering on a strategy.

Insight or Value Created

Kaplan and Norton argue that the balanced scorecard "gives managers a way of ensuring that all levels of the organization understand the long-term strategy and that both departmental and individual objectives are aligned with it."[5]

The scorecard provides a means to measure and monitor diverse factors that are associated with successful strategy implementation. The balanced scorecard tends to be generic enough that the overall structure can be used in different industry contexts, but in each context and firm it can also be adapted to meet the needs of that firm.

It provides a holistic way to set objectives that align with the strategy but impact different elements of the organization. It also provides a way to monitor the performance of the organization over time, so that objectives that align with the overall strategy are achieved. It is therefore a useful way to break down a strategy from something that is abstract to something that is concrete and actionable.

Risks and Limitations

One criticism of the balanced scorecard is that it does not provide a bottom-line score or a unified view with clear recommendations; it is simply a list of metrics. Managers need to act on those metrics to make them useful, and in some cases, managers may be too busy, too distracted, or too unmotivated to pay attention to the metrics and use them as a basis for action.

A second criticism of the balanced scorecard is that the model fails to fully reflect the needs of diverse stakeholders—favoring financial stakeholders over others. Even though the model provides a balanced perspective, it is designed to drive financial returns. This may be done at the expense of communities, the environment, suppliers, or other key stakeholders. Using the balanced scorecard approach may blind managers to these important issues.

The number of objectives and metrics created by a balanced scorecard may also be problematic. Many times, a firm implementing a balanced scorecard approach to implementing strategy will end up with twenty objectives, measures, targets, and initiatives. This is a lot for a management team to keep track of, and there are scholars who argue for simpler approaches, suggesting that there is benefit to trading detail for simplicity.

Case Illustration: The Chocolate Moose

Context

In the chapter on SWOT analysis (Chapter 11), we introduced the case of the Chocolate Moose, the independently owned and operated ice cream shop located in the college town of Bloomington, Indiana. As discussed, two significant external events in the spring of 2015 became a cause of concern for the Chocolate Moose's owners. First, their landlord informed them that he intended to sell the parcel of land on which their store and production facility were located. Second, the City of Bloomington had just recently announced plans to modernize the downtown area, including widening and repaving the street the store called home. For most of the next three years, the only way to access the parking lot would be on foot. Combined, these two events would inevitably lead to a decline in business, and the owners needed to generate strategic growth recommendations that would avert the end of the iconic ice cream shop in this college town.

The owners of the Chocolate Moose decided to double down on their strength in local ice cream retail. They leveraged the nostalgic brand of the original store and opened two new retail locations: one new retail store to replace the old store in downtown Bloomington and a second store in the downtown area of the neighboring community of Nashville, Indiana. The two stores were a mere twenty miles apart, and the strength of the brand translated easily to the new location. With a much greater investment in their retail locations, they needed to very carefully deliver on their new strategy. One means of doing this is via the balanced scorecard.

Developing and Implementing a Balanced Scorecard

Step 1. Articulate the vision and strategy of the firm. The vision for the business is to be the premium local producer and retailer of ice cream in south-central Indiana, to be a retail destination where people of all ages go to get the best ice cream. The strategy underlying this vision entails (1) controlling the production of ice cream and only using the highest-quality, most flavorful ingredients for all ice cream production; (2) producing an array of exciting, novel flavors of ice cream; (3) providing a fun, inviting, and clean retail space, where customers feel welcome and want to hang out; and (4) growing the business by offering catering services to provide premium ice cream at local events.

Steps 2 and 3. Transform the vision and strategy of the firm into objectives for each element of the scorecard—learning and growth, internal business processes, customers, and finances. Specify the measures, targets, and initiatives for each of the objectives under each perspective in the balanced scorecard. This should translate into fifteen to twenty objectives, measures, targets, and initiatives within a firm. Table 20.2 outlines the objectives, measures, targets, and initiatives for the Chocolate Moose as it attempts to implement its strategic initiatives.

Table 20.2 Balanced Scorecard Objectives, Measures, Targets, and Initiatives for the Chocolate Moose

Area	Objectives	Measures	Targets	Initiatives
Learning and growth	Make the Chocolate Moose a great place to work	Employee satisfaction (measured monthly with quick survey); employee turnover measured annually	Employee satisfaction score >90%; employee turnover <20% per annum	Weekly meeting with employees to assess status; managers to know each employee's name, interests, and preferences

Table 20.2 Continued

Area	Objectives	Measures	Targets	Initiatives
	Get employees to contribute back to their fellow workers	# of employee contribution projects or initiatives per year	Six employee contribution projects or initiatives per year	Allow employees to initiate and manage projects at work
Internal business processes	Minimize waste	Spoiled inventory percentage	Spoiled inventory percentage <5% each month	Train employees on how to minimize waste; maintain all equipment
	Employees continually improve the operations of the business	# of employee suggestions/ improvements	Six new employee suggestions per month	Employee suggestion text line; employee sharing sessions
Customers	Happy customers	Customer compliment-to-complaint ratio	Customer compliment-to-complaint ratio of five to one	Customer service training; customer service reminders/ cues in stores
	Positive word of mouth and social sharing	Sentiment analysis of posts on social media	Positive-to-negative sentiment ratio of five to one	Engage customers online—post to social media channels daily
Financial	Revenue growth	Comparable month review growth over prior year	15% comparable month revenue growth, year over year	Social media marketing campaign; ongoing marketing initiative
	Profit margins	Annual profit margin percentage	20% annual net profit margin	Cost management monthly review

Step 4. Monitor performance of each initiative according to the targets, measures, and objectives that have been set. With the objectives, measures, targets, and initiatives in place, the owners of the Chocolate Moose need to ensure that everything in the balanced scorecard is shared with all employees and other relevant stakeholders. Then, on a monthly basis, the performance of the firm on each different dimension can be assessed in relation to each target and course corrections made where measures are lagging the targets.

In this way, the strategy of the firm can be carefully implemented, measured, and monitored so that the desired results can be achieved.

21
Conclusion

Coming Full Circle

We wrote this book with a set of clear a priori assumptions about the field of strategy. These outline our view on the role of strategy in the uncertain, fast-paced world that we live in:

- The field of strategy in the current day and age has become more relevant (*not* less).
- It should be practiced by more people (*not* fewer, and certainly *not* solely by those at the top of the organization.
- Its functional domain should be broadened (*not* narrowed).
- *Anyone* with career ambition in the business world needs to become a strategist.

These assumptions outline both our motivation for and our ambition with writing this book.

It is not rare for us to come across people in search of a book that is both practical and well grounded, that discusses tools and concepts that real people can use for real problems even if they don't reside in the C-suite, and that offers practical, easy-to-follow, step-by-step advice. This is the book we meant to write, and we hope that it will be a useful resource for those wanting to become strategists, and to help those who already are strategists to become better ones.

The 3D Framework in Action

To strategize, one must continuously diagnose, decide, and deliver. The tools that form the body and soul of our framework aid in navigating this process. We structured the book by offering tools that assist with each stage, recognizing that some tools can be used for multiple stages (the "heat map" on p. 37 illuminated the differences).

Something we have not yet discussed is that tools, in practice, are rarely used in isolation (even though, for explanatory purposes, our chapters were written this way). As the saying goes, when your only tool is a hammer, every problem looks like a nail. The kinds of problems companies face nowadays, however, rarely resemble just "nails." Consequently, strategists tend to apply a broader toolkit than just hammers.

There are no hard-and-fast rules when it comes to applying tools in tandem. What does stand out, though, is that making combinations that "click" with the specific problem in focus adds more value than simply adding tools in isolation. For example, one of our students (who worked as a middle manager at a major European manufacturing firm) was struggling with the question of whether her company should enter a new, adjacent industry. To answer this question, the student applied five-forces analysis to gauge the profit potential of the new space. However, she also wanted to know whether the company's unique strengths fit with this new space, as well as the customer needs the company would face in that new market. For this reason, she applied VRIO analysis to her own company, detecting which of the resources it held were truly valuable, then overlapping this with the knowledge about the new market she developed using five forces.

When she had decided, after this diagnosis, that she was going to recommend to the board that the company enter the new market, she performed a market entry modes analysis to determine the optimal method by which this could be achieved.

While this example may be unique in the sense that it illustrates a particular problem faced by a particular strategist, it does offer some insight with regard to combining tools:

1. *Let the problem define the parameters.* What we mean by this is that preconceived preferences for certain tools or frameworks

offer less useful insights than the application of tools specifically developed to address certain problems. In other words, start from the problem or question you face. Then let this guide the selection of the most appropriate tools you apply.

2. *Combine tools that offer complementary insights.* No two tools overlap *exactly*, but some are more alike than others. Taking the first point of advice into account, it makes sense to select tools that will investigate different sides of a problem, making sure no stone is left unturned.

3. Oftentimes (unless for very specific strategic problems) it makes sense to *include at least one external and one internal tool in tandem.* Few strategic questions are truly only internal or only external. Take the example we just presented about the manufacturing firm wanting to gauge whether entering a specific new market would be a good strategic move. Of course, we want to know generally whether this new market is attractive, but the more important question is whether the market is also *attractive for us.* So, answering this question requires some combination of external and internal analysis (five forces and VRIO analysis, respectively, in this example).

Again, there is no magic set of combinations that always works. If there were, we would not withhold that information. Part of the learning experience in becoming a good strategist is learning when and how to apply certain tools in combination. As with many things in life, practice makes perfect.

The Next Frontier

As we repeated time and time again, strategy, to us, is about diagnosing the diverse array of complex challenges confronting organizations, deciding on novel solutions to address those challenges, and delivering by taking action on those solutions. This is the framework that we advocate in this book, and the framework that has provided us, and our students, the most benefit.

At the same time, we should acknowledge that the process of strategy formulation in practice is often messier than what is depicted here. Mintzberg's work has reminded us that firms sometimes stumble onto successful strategies through a more emergent process.[1] Our work aligns with Mintzberg's in the sense that we also believe strategy should not be a top-down process, or one initiated by, or exclusive to, those at the top of the organization. Strategists are everywhere. So, we are aligned in our dismissal of the view of the chief executive officer as the almighty, all-knowing strategy designer.

Still, and this is where we may differ, we maintain that understanding the structure and logic behind the 3D process can help managers and employees navigate and bring some structure to messier, more organic strategy formulation processes. Our framework is not meant to be followed slavishly, but to inspire a sense of purpose and direction. It also forces us to look at problems through multiple lenses and from multiple perspectives. In that sense, it truly allows viewing strategy in 3D.

Notes

Chapter 2

1. Andrews, K., *The Concept of Corporate Strategy* (Homewood, IL: Richard D. Irwin, 1971).
2. Porter, M., *Competitive Strategy: Techniques for Analyzing Competitors* (New York: Free Press, 1980).
3. Rumelt, R., *Good Strategy Bad Strategy* (New York: Crown Business, 2011).
4. Lafley, A. G., & Martin, R., *Playing to Win: How Strategy Really Works* (Cambridge, MA: Harvard Business Press, 2013).

Chapter 3

1. Hill, C. W. L., Jones, G. R., & Schilling, M. A., *Strategic Management: Theory* (Stamford, CT: Cengage Learning, 2015).
2. Rothaermel, F. T., *Strategic Management* (New York, NY: McGraw-Hill Education, 2015).
3. Ibid.
4. From http://www.mckinsey.com/about-us/what-we-do/our-mission-and-values (accessed July 31, 2017).
5. Ibid.
6. Prahalad, C. K., & Hamel, G., The core competence of the corporation, *Harvard Business Review* (1990) 68(3): 79–91
7. Rumelt, R., *Good Strategy Bad Strategy* (New York, NY: Crown Business, 2011).
8. Magretta, J., *Understanding Michel Porter* (Cambridge, MA: Harvard Business Press, 2012).
9. Barney, J., & Hesterley, W., *Strategic Management and Competitive Advantage* (Hoboken, NJ: Pearson, 2015).
10. Hill, C., Jones, G., & Schilling, M., *Strategic Management* (Stamford, CT: Cengage Learning, 2015).

Chapter 4

1. Ohno, T., *Toyota Production System: Beyond Large-Scale Production* (Boca Raton, FL: CRC Press, 1988).
2. Mintzberg, H., Raisinghani, D., & Theoret, A., The structure of unstructured decision processes, *Administrative Science Quarterly* (1976) 21: 246–275.
3. Simon, H. A., Rational choice and the structure of the environment, *Psychological Review* (1976) 63: 129–138.

Chapter 5

1. Christensen, C., Hall, T., Dillon, K., & Duncan, D., *Competing Against Luck: The Story of Innovation and Customer Choice* (Cambridge, MA: Harvard Business School Publishing, 2016).

Chapter 6

1. Pfeffer, J., & Salancik, G., *The External Control of Organizations: A Resource Dependence Perspective* (Palo Alto, CA: Stanford University Press, 2003).
2. Hannan, M. T., & Freeman, J., The population ecology of organizations, *American Journal of Sociology* (1977) 82(5): 929–964.
3. Fleisher, C. S., & Bensoussan, B. E., *Strategic and Competitive Analysis: Methods and Techniques for Analyzing Business Competition* (Upper Saddle River, NJ: Prentice Hall, 2003) (p. 269).
4. Pfeffer, J., & Salancik, G., *The External Control of Organizations: A Resource Dependence Perspective* (Palo Alto, CA: Stanford University Press, 2003).
5. https://rapidbi.com/history-of-pest-analysis/ (accessed July 31, 2017).
6. Fleisher, C. S., & Bensoussan, B. E., *Strategic and Competitive Analysis: Methods and Techniques for Analyzing Business Competition* (Upper Saddle River, NJ: Prentice Hall, 2003) (p. 269).

Chapter 7

1. Porter, M., How competitive forces shape strategy, *Harvard Business Review* (1979) 57(2): 137–145.
2. Porter, M., The five competitive forces that shape strategy, *Harvard Business Review* (2008) 86(1): 25–40.
3. Adapted from Porter, M. E.. The five competitive forces that shape strategy. *Harvard Business Review*, (2008) 86(1), 25–40.
4. Adapted from Magretta, J. *Understanding Michael Porter: The essential guide to competition and strategy.* (Boston, MA: Harvard Business Review Press, 2012) (p.56–57).

5. Adapted from Magretta, J. *Understanding Michael Porter: The essential guide to competition and strategy.* (Boston, MA: Harvard Business Review Press, 2012) (p.61).
6. Harley-Davidson targets new consumers, *FT Business*, February 22, 2016.
7. https://csimarket.com/stocks/competition2.php?supply&code=HOG (accessed August 8, 2019).
8. Harley-Davidson: An overreliance on aging baby boomers, Rotterdam School of Management Case Development Center, Erasmus University (2014).
9. Ibid.
10. Harley-Davidson needs a new generation of riders, *Bloomberg Business Week*, August 23, 2018.
11. Harley-Davidson: An overreliance on aging baby boomers, Rotterdam School of Management Case Development Center, Erasmus University (2014).
12. Roese, N. J. & Kompella, M. *Harley-Davidson: Chasing a New Generation of Customers* (Evanston, IL: Kellogg School of Management, Northwestern University, 2013).
13. Harley-Davidson closes Missouri plant as shipments slump, shares fall, *Reuters*, January 30, 2018.

Chapter 8

1. Porter, M., *Competitive Strategy: Techniques for Analyzing Industries and Competitors* (New York: Free Press, 1980).
2. Porter, M., *Competitive Advantage: Creating and Sustaining Superior Advantage* (New York: Free Press, 1985).
3. Fleisher, C. S., & Bensoussan, B. E., *Strategic and Competitive Analysis: Methods and Techniques for Analyzing Business Competition* (Upper Saddle River, NJ: Prentice Hall, 2003).
4. Ibid.
5. Adapted from Porter M. E. *Competitive strategy.* (New York: Free Press, 1980).
6. Thompson, A. A., Netflix' strategy in 2018: Does the company have sufficient competitive strength to fight off aggressive rivals? In: Gamble, J. E., Peteraf, M., & Thompson, A. A. (eds.), *Essentials of Strategic Management: The Quest for Competitive Advantage* (6th ed.) (New York, NY: McGraw-Hill, 2019).
7. Ibid.
8. Ibid.
9. https://nscreenmedia.com/2018-hulu-performance-soars-losses-continue/ (accessed May 17, 2019).
10. https://www.techradar.com/news/disney-plus-vs-netflix-who-will-win (accessed May 20, 2019).
11. We will return to this theme in the illustration of value chain analysis in Chapter 14.

Chapter 9

1. Wernerfelt, B., A resource-based view of the firm, *Strategic Management Journal* (1984) 5: 171–180.
2. Barney, J., Firm resources and sustained competitive advantage, *Journal of Management* (1991) 17(1): 99–120.
3. Rumelt, R. P., Towards a strategic theory of the firm. In Lamb, R. (ed.), *Competitive Strategic Management* (Englewood Cliffs, NJ: Prentice Hall, 1984) (pp. 556–570).
4. Wernerfelt, B., A resource-based view of the firm, *Strategic Management Journal* (1984) 5: 171–180.
5. Priem, R. L., & Butler, J. E. Is the resource-based "view" a useful perspective for strategic management research?, *Academy of Management Review* (2001) 26(1): 22–40.
6. Barney, J., Firm resources and sustained competitive advantage, *Journal of Management* (1991) 17(1): 99–120.
7. Hofer, C. W., & Schendel, D., *Strategy Formulation: Analytic Concepts* (St. Paul, MN: West, 1978).
8. Adapted from Rothaermel (2015).
9. Barney, J., & Hesterley, W., *Strategic Management and Competitive Advantage* (Hoboken, NJ: Pearson, 2015).
10. Teece, D. J., Pisano, G., & Shuen, A., Dynamic capabilities and strategic management, *Strategic Management Journal* (1997) 18(7): 509–533.
11. Knott, P. J., Does VRIO help managers evaluate a firm's resources?, *Management Decision* (2015) 53(8): 1806–1822.
12. Harley-Davidson needs a new generation of riders, *Bloomberg Business Week*, August 23, 2018.
13. Quoted in ibid.
14. Harley-Davidson: An overreliance on aging baby boomers, Rotterdam School of Management Case Development Center, Erasmus University (2014).
15. Harley-Davidson needs a new generation of riders, *Bloomberg Business Week*, August 23, 2018.

Chapter 10

1. Metcalf, R. W., & Titard, P. L., *Principles of Accounting* (Philadelphia, PA: WB Saunders Company, 1976).
2. Adapted from Lewellen, W. G., Halloran, J. A., & Lanser, H. P., *Financial Management: An Introduction to Principles and Practice* (Boston, MA: Western College Publishing, 2000).
3. https://www.beveragedaily.com/Article/2013/11/13/Indra-Nooyi-laughs-off-irrelevant-Pepsi-v-Coke-competition-talk# (accessed May 20, 2019).

Chapter 11

1. Helms, M. M., & Nixon, J., Exploring SWOT analysis—Where are we now? A review of academic research from the last decade, *Journal of Strategy and Management* (2010) 3(3): 215–251.
2. Learned, E. P., Christiansen, C. R., Andrews, K., & Guth, W. D., *Business Policy: Text and Cases* (Homewood, IL: Irwin, 1969).
3. Grant, R. M., Why strategy teaching should be theory based, *Journal of Management Inquiry* (2008) 17(4): 276–291.
4. Valentin, E. K., SWOT analysis from a resource-based view, *Journal of Marketing Theory and Practice* (2001) 9(2): 54–69.
5. Panagiotou, G., Bringing SWOT into focus, *Business Strategy Review* (2003) 24(2): 8–16.
6. Helms, M. M., & Nixon, J., Exploring SWOT analysis—Where are we now? A review of academic research from the last decade, *Journal of Strategy and Management* (2010) 3(3): 215–251.

Chapter 12

1. Deming, W., *Out of the Crisis* (Cambridge, MA: Massachusetts Institute of Technology, Center for Advanced Engineering Study, 1986)

Chapter 13

1. Kuznets, S., *Secular Movements in Production and Prices* (Boston: Houghton Mifflin, 1930).
2. Fleisher, C. S., & Bensoussan, B. E., *Strategic and Competitive Analysis: Methods and Techniques for Analyzing Business Competition* (Upper Saddle River, NJ: Prentice Hall, 2003).
3. Levitt, T., Exploit the product life cycle, *Harvard Business Review* (1965) November–December: 81–94.
4. Moore, G., *Crossing the Chasm* (New York: HarperCollins Publishers, 2006).

Chapter 14

1. Porter, M. E., *Competitive Advantage* (New York: Free Press, 1985).
2. Hergert, M., & Morris, D., Accounting data for value chain analysis, *Strategic Management Journal* (1989) 10: 175–188.
3. Ibid.

4. The third generic strategy mentioned by Porter—focus—is often distinguished from cost leadership and differentiation given the different level of analysis it applies to. See Murray, A. I., A contingency view of Porter's "generic strategies," *Academy of Management Review* (1988) 13(3): 390–400.

5. Dess, G. G., & Davis, P. S., Porter's (1980) generic strategies as determinants of strategic group membership, *Academy of Management Journal* (1984) 27(3): 467–488.

6. Porter, M. E., *Competitive Strategy* (New York: Free Press, 1980).

7. Hergert, M., & Morris, D., Accounting data for value chain analysis, *Strategic Management Journal* (1989) 10: 175–188.

8. Fleisher, C. S., & Bensoussan, B. E., *Strategic and Competitive Analysis: Methods and Techniques for Analyzing Business Competition* (Upper Saddle River, NJ: Prentice Hall, 2003) (p. 269).

9. Ibid.

10. Adapted from McIvor, R., What is the right outsourcing strategy for your process?, *European Management Journal* (2008) 26: 24–34.

11. Adapted from Porter, M. E., *Competitive Advantage* (New York: Free Press, 1985).

12. Fleisher, C. S., & Bensoussan, B. E., *Strategic and Competitive Analysis: Methods and Techniques for Analyzing Business Competition* (Upper Saddle River, NJ: Prentice Hall, 2003).

13. Hergert, M., & Morris, D., Accounting data for value chain analysis, *Strategic Management Journal* (1989) 10: 175–188.

14. Ibid.

15. Merchant, N., Why Porter's model no longer works, *Harvard Business Review*, Blog network, February 29, 2012, https://hbr.org/2012/02/why-porters-model-no-longer-wo.

16. Ibid.

17. Rothaermel, F.T., & Guenther, A., Netflix, Inc. In: Rothaermel, F.T. (ed.), *Strategic Management: Concepts & Cases* (New York, NY: McGraw-Hill, 2015).

18. https://www.theverge.com/2018/12/18/18146186/att-time-warner-streaming-video-net-neutrality (accessed January 21, 2019).

Chapter 15

1. This is the original process for applying hypothesis testing in business decision-making scenarios. There is an alternative hypothesis-testing approach that has been developed by Proctor & Gamble. This alternative approach is elaborated upon in the following article: Lafley, A. G., Martin, R. L., Rivkin, J. W., & Siggelkow, N., Bringing science to the art of strategy, *Harvard Business Review* (2012) 90(9): 3–12.

Chapter 16

1. Madhavaram, S., & Hunt, S. D., The service-dominant logic and a hierarchy of operant resources: Developing masterful operant resources and implications for marketing strategy, *Journal of the Academy of Marketing Science* (2008) 36(1): 67–82

2. Dickson, P. R., & Ginter, J. L., Market segmentation, product differentiation, and marketing strategy, *Journal of Marketing* (1987) 51(2): 1–10.

3. Mittal, V., & Kamakura, W. A., Satisfaction, repurchase intent, and repurchase behavior: Investigating the moderating effect of customer characteristics. *Journal of Marketing Research*, (2001) 38(1): 131–142.

4. Wernerfelt, B., A resource-based view of the firm, *Strategic Management Journal* (1984) 5: 171–180.

5. Priem, R. L., & Butler, J. E., Is the resource-based "view" a useful perspective for strategic management research?, *Academy of Management Review* (2001) 26(1): 22–40.

6. Gavett, G., What you need to know about segmentation, *Harvard Business Review*, Online: July 9, 2014, https://hbr.org/2014/07/what-you-need-to-know-about-segmentation.

7. Harley-Davidson needs a new generation of riders, *Bloomberg Business Week*, August 23, 2018.

8. Harley-Davidson: An overreliance on aging baby boomers, Rotterdam School of Management Case Development Center, Erasmus University (2014).

9. Harley-Davidson closes Missouri plant as shipments slump, shares fall, *Reuters*, January 30, 2018.

10. Harley-Davidson: An overreliance on aging baby boomers, Rotterdam School of Management Case development Center, Erasmus University (2014).

11. Harley-Davidson needs a new generation of riders, *Bloomberg Business Week*, August 23, 2018.

12. Ibid.

13. Ibid.

14. Ibid.

15. Ibid.

16. Ibid.

17. Ibid.

Chapter 17

1. http://economistsview.typepad.com/economistsview/2009/10/transaction-cost-economics.html (accessed July 31, 2017).

2. Adapted from Casadesus-Masanell, R., Tarziján, J. & Mitchell, J.. Teaching Note: Arauco (A) and (B). *Harvard Business School Publishing,* (2010) Product #: 5-706-439.
3. Stuckey, J., & White, D. When and when not to vertically integrate. *MIT Sloan Management Review,* (1993) 34(3): 71–83.
4. See Jargon, J., Starbucks buys its first coffee farm, *Wall Street Journal,* https://www.wsj.com/articles/SB10001424127887323639604578368741173186364.
5. Michael Roberto blog, http://michael-roberto.blogspot.com/2013/03/backward-integration-at-starbucks.html (accessed April 30, 2019).

Chapter 18

1. Anderson, E., & Gatignon, H., Modes of foreign entry: A transaction cost analysis and propositions, *Journal of International Business Studies* (1986) 17(3): 1–26.
2. Hill, C. W., Hwang, P., & Kim, W. C., An eclectic theory of the choice of international entry mode, *Strategic Management Journal* (1990) 11(2): 117–128.
3. Kotha, S., & Glassman, D., *Starbucks Corporation: Competing in a Global Market* (Seattle, WA: UW Business School Case Study, 2003). Accessed at https://sureshkotha.files.wordpress.com/2018/05/starbucks_intl-copy1.pdf.
4. Ibid.

Chapter 19

1. Osterwalder, A., *The Business Model Ontology: A Proposition in a Design Science Approach* (2004) (accessed July 31, 2017 at https://serval.unil.ch/resource/serval:BIB_R_4210.P001/REF.pdf).
2. Buckminster Fuller, R., *Cosmography: A Posthumous Scenario for the Future of Humanity* (Hoboken, NJ: Hungry Minds [Wiley], 1992).
3. March, S. T., & Smith, G. F., Design and natural science research on information technology, *Decision Support Systems* (1995) 15(4): 251–266.
4. Osterwalder, A., *The Business Model Ontology: A Proposition in a Design Science Approach* (2004) (accessed July 31, 2017 at https://serval.unil.ch/resource/serval:BIB_R_4210.P001/REF.pdf).
5. Kaplan, R. S., & Norton, D. P., The balanced scorecard—measures that drive performance, *Harvard Business Review* (1992) 70(1): 71–79.
6. Markides, C., *All the Right Moves* (Cambridge, MA: Harvard Business School Press, 1999).

7. Adapted from Osterwalder, A., & Pigneur, Y., *Business Model Generation: A Handbook for Visionaries, Game Changers, and Challengers.* (Hoboken, NJ: John Wiley & Sons, 2010).

Chapter 20

1. Drucker, P., *The Practice of Management* (New York: HarperCollins, 1954).
2. Kaplan, R. S., & Norton, D. P., The balanced scorecard—measures that drive performance, *Harvard Business Review* (1992) 70(1): 71–79.
3. Kaplan, R. S., Conceptual foundations of the balanced scorecard, *Handbooks of Management Accounting Research* (2009) 3: 1253–1269.
4. Adapted from Kaplan, R. S., & Norton, D. P., The balanced scorecard—measures that drive performance, *Harvard Business Review* (1992) 70(1): 71–79.
5. Kaplan, R. S., & Norton, D. P. Using the balanced scorecard as a strategic management system. *Harvard Business Review* (1996), 74(1): 75–85, p. 76

Chapter 21

1. Mintzberg, H., *The Rise and Fall of Strategic Planning*, (New York, NY: Simon and Schuster, 1994).

Index

Note: Tables, figures and boxes are indicated by *t*, *f* and *b* following the page number

For the benefit of digital users, indexed terms that span two pages (e.g., 52–53) may, on occasion, appear on only one of those pages.

CPSIA information can be obtained
at www.ICGtesting.com
Printed in the USA
BVHW040539100122
625812BV00003B/6

9 780190 081485